AF605795

Yudisher Theriak

Yudisher Theriak

An Early Modern Yiddish Defense of Judaism

EDITED AND TRANSLATED
BY MORRIS M. FAIERSTEIN

Wayne State University Press | Detroit

20 19 18 17 16 5 4 3 2 1

ISBN 978–0-8143–4248–0 (hardcover)
ISBN 978–0-8143–4249–7 (ebook)

Library of Congress Cataloging Number:
2016953020

Designed and typeset by Sandy Freeman
Composed in Adobe Caslon Pro

Wayne State University Press
Leonard N. Simons Building
4809 Woodward Avenue
Detroit, Michigan 48201-1309

Visit us online at wsupress.wayne.edu

For my in-laws,

Mort and Eloise Eckhouse,

With Love and Affection

Contents

Preface

The *Yudisher Theriak* (Jewish Theriac [1615]), by Zalman Zvi of Aufhausen, is a unique work. It is the only Jewish book written in Yiddish that responds to the many anti-Jewish polemics written by Christians and Jewish converts to Christianity in early modern Germany. Though originally written as a response to a specific text, *Jüdischer abgestreiffter Schlangenbalg* (Jewish Stripped-off Snakeskin [1614]), by Samuel Friedrich Brenz, a Jewish convert to Christianity, it presents an interesting picture of how a learned Jew who was not a member of the rabbinic elite might respond to the many accusations against Jews and Judaism that became standardized and were repeated from author to author. The *Yudisher Theriak* makes a passing appearance in many scholarly books and articles written about Christian-Jewish relations in early modern Germany. Its existence is acknowledged, and occasionally a fact or idea is cited from it, but its arguments and ideas have not been integrated into the scholarly literature on this subject.

One reason that the *Yudisher Theriak* has not received the attention it deserves is its language. It is written in a form of early modern Yiddish—more influenced by German than its contemporary East European variant—that is difficult for readers who are not familiar with it. In addition, the author, Zalman Zvi of Aufhausen, was a learned Jew who interspersed Hebrew phrases, rabbinic terminology, and allusions to rabbinic literature in his work. My goal in this book is more modest than elucidating all the references and allusions in the scholarly literature that are included in this book. Rather, it is to make this text available in an annotated translation that will serve as a useful tool for scholars and students of Jewish-Christian relations in the early modern period and, more broadly, for early modern Jewish historical and cultural studies. The analysis and clarification of the many issues raised in the *Yudisher Theriak* await further studies. This book attempts to take the first step by making it accessible to an audience beyond the very narrow band of specialists in early modern Yiddish literature.

There were defenses of Judaism in early modern Italy, the most famous of which was *Historia de' riti hebraici*, by Rabbi Leon Modena of Venice (1571–1648). It was first published in Paris in 1637, and subsequently translated and reprinted many times. However, there were significant cultural and legal differences between German and Italian Jewry during that period. Similarly, on the individual level, there are significant differences between writers who were members of the cultural and intellectual elite, including Modena and the Christian Hebraist scholar Johannes Buxtorf of Basel (1564–1629), author of *Judenschul* (Basel, 1623), on one hand, and Zalman Zvi of Aufhausen and Samuel Friedrich Brenz on the other. Undoubtedly many other issues will come to light with the publication of the *Yudisher Theriak*, an important but neglected text.

Several friends shared their knowledge with me and responded to various queries while I was working on this project. My thanks to Pfarrer Helmut Foth, Rabbi Rebecca Kushner, and Rabbi Jerry Schwarzbard for their friendship and assistance with this and other projects. The anonymous readers for the press read the manuscript carefully and offered many comments and suggestions that contributed to improving the quality of this work; my thanks to them for their efforts. Finally and most important, the love and support of my spouse, Ruth Anne Faierstein, has given me the spiritual strength to pursue my scholarly interests.

My thanks to Kathryn Wildfong, editor-in-chief of Wayne State University Press, and members of her staff for their invaluable assistance in bringing this work to publication.

Rockville, Maryland

Introduction

The *Yudisher Theriak* (Jewish Theriac) by Zalman Zvi of Aufhausen, first published in Hanau in 1615, was a response to an anti-Jewish work entitled *Jüdischer abgestreiffter Schlangenbalg* (Jewish Stripped-off Snakeskin), by Samuel Friedrich Brenz, a Jewish convert to Christianity, which had been published in Nürnberg and Augsburg in 1614.[1] Brenz's volume was part of a genre of anti-Jewish books and pamphlets, written in German and addressed to Christians, which purported to reveal how Jews mocked and blasphemed against the Christian religion, cursed their Christian neighbors, and engaged in magic and witchcraft to inflict damage on the Christians' possessions and livelihoods.

Johannes Pfefferkorn's small book *Der Juden veindt*, first published in 1509, was one of the earliest examples of this genre of anti-Jewish literature.[2] Though Pfefferkorn was Catholic, many Protestants adopted his ideas about the importance of blasphemy and the Jews after the Protestant Reformation, and his small volume became a model for many later works of this type.

Unlike Brenz's polemic, which was part of a well-defined genre of anti-Jewish literature, Zalman Zvi's *Yudisher Theriak* was unique. It was the only Jewish book published in Germany—and in Yiddish, the Jewish

1. A detailed publication history of both works can be found in Appendix 1.
2. The full title of the work is *Ich bin ein buchlein Der Juden veindt ist mein namen* (I am a Small Book: The Enemy of the Jews Is My Name). It was first published in Cologne in 1509. An analysis of this work can be found in Ellen Martin, *Die deutsche Schriften des Johannes Pfefferkorn: Zum Problem des Judenhasses und der Intoleranz in der Zeit der Vorreformation* (Göppingen: Kümmerle, 1994), 115–31. See also Hans-Martin Kirn, *Das Bild vom Juden im Deutschland des frühen 16. Jahrhunderts: Dargestellt an den Schriften Johannes Pfefferkorns* (Tübingen: Mohr Siebeck, 1989).

vernacular—to directly respond to the attacks on Jews and Judaism in the early modern period. It responded to Brenz's assertions accusation by accusation and paragraph by paragraph. Even his choice of title was a refutation of Brenz's imagery. Brenz suggested with his title that he would strip off the skin of the Jewish snake to expose the Jewish evil.[3] In response Zalman Zvi suggested that his book would be the antidote to the snake venom that was being spewed by Brenz.

Zalman Zvi's title, *Yudisher Theriak*, has a twofold resonance. Not only was it a direct allusion to Brenz's title, but it also hinted at a larger purpose. The term *theriac* is a Greek and Latin term for the antidote to the bite of a venomous snake. It is also found in the Talmud, where it has the same meaning.[4] In the sixteenth and seventeenth centuries, the term was used for the Galenic universal cure, which enjoyed a wide popularity during this period. As Andrew Pettegree writes, "All cities with a university or medical college prepared their own theriac, often in a civic public ceremony involving magistrates, physicians and ecclesiastical dignitaries. . . . Venice abandoned its public ceremony for the mixing of theriac only in 1842."[5] It is possible that Zalman Zvi was familiar with the contemporaneous significance of the term *theriac*.[6] Perhaps he hoped that his book would also serve as a theriac for the scourge of anti-Judaism that was prevalent in his generation.[7]

ZALMAN ZVI OF AUFHAUSEN

Zalman Zvi tells us on the title page of his *Theriak* that he came from the town of Aufhausen, under the Schenkenstein.[8] With one exception, the information that we have about Zalman Zvi comes from what can be gleaned from scattered comments in the *Theriak*.[9] Information about his

3. The text of Brenz's title page can be found in Appendix 1.
4. B. *Shabbat* 109b and B. *Nedarim* 41b.
5. Andrew Pettegree, *The Book in the Renaissance* (New Haven, CT: Yale University Press, 2010), 317.
6. As we will see, we know that he spent time in Italy, and he may well have witnessed one of these theriac ceremonies.
7. As will be discussed, Zalman Zvi hoped to publish a German version of his book for a Christian audience but ultimately was not able to do so.
8. This is Burg Schenkenstein, a castle that sits above the village of Aufhausen, which today is a suburb of the city of Bopfingen (Ostalbkreis) in Baden Württemberg, near the Bavarian border.
9. There are some documents relating to Zalman Zvi's efforts to publish his book for Christians in Hanau. This will be discussed later in the book.

life is sketchy. He had a wife and six children, whom he mentions having left behind in great destitution for almost a year in order to write his book, which required much travel and financial expenditure. He was a *mohel*[10] by profession and possibly also a ritual slaughterer (*shohet*).[11] Zalman Zvi mentions that he had to take an official oath under very aggravating circumstances.[12] This is most probably a reference to the "More Judaico," an oath Jews were compelled to take in the course of lawsuits with non-Jews. This would indicate that he had some sort of serious legal or financial difficulty.[13]

In the introduction he speaks of suffering and misfortune; evil Jews took away what was his and chased him away so that he was forced to move to foreign lands and wander for many years. He explicitly mentions that he had been in Italy,[14] and scattered references indicate some knowledge of Italian language and culture. For example, he knows the meaning and derivation of the term *pope* and knows the meaning of *duomo*.[15] He also alludes to the local practices in a number of countries at various points in his work, but it is not clear if he speaks from firsthand experience or based on what he had heard from others or from reading.

Zalman Zvi's high level of Jewish education is on display throughout the book. He opens the volume with an elaborate poem written in the specific style of religious poetry that is full of biblical verses and allusions to verses.[16] He cites rabbinic texts on numerous occasions and often gives specific references, including the Talmudic tractate and specific page of the passage he is quoting. When I checked these citations, I found them

---

10. A ritual circumciser. *Yudisher Theriak* 4.23. The *Yudisher Theriak* (hereafter *Theriak*) is divided into an introduction and seven chapters. Each paragraph within each chapter is numbered. Thus I have adopted the citation system of citing a passage by chapter and paragraph number. This system is used both in the *Schlangenbalg* and in the Yiddish editions of the *Theriak*, and thus simplifies cross-references among the different texts.

11. This possibility is suggested by the circumstances of a story recounted in *Theriak* 4.12 about meat that was not kosher. The two professions of *shohet* and *mohel* often went together, so the supposition is reasonable.

12. *Theriak* 3.9.

13. On this oath, see Isaac Levitats, "Oath More Judaico or Jurametum Judaeorum," *Encyclopedia Judaica* (Jerusalem: Keter, 1971), 1302–3.

14. *Theriak* 2.31.

15. *Pope* (*Theriak* 2.5); *duomo* (*Theriak* 2.20).

16. It is in the *Azharot* style, a type of *piyyut* for *Shavuot*. See Israel Zinberg, *History of Jewish Literature: Old Yiddish Literature from Its Origins to the Haskalah Period*, vol. 7 (Cincinnati: Hebrew Union College Press, 1975), 165.

generally to be accurate. (The few discrepancies I found are indicated in the footnotes.) Thus he had a solid rabbinic education that was not unusual for a member of the secondary rabbinic intelligentsia of that period.[17]

What was very rare about Zalman Zvi as a German Jew of his time was his knowledge of written German, which was more than adequate for him to read and understand works written in German. To begin with he read, digested, and wrote a point-by-point refutation of Brenz's *Schlangenbalg*. Even more impressive are the many works in German with which he was familiar. He cites the New Testament twenty-five times, often citing specific chapters and verses.[18] In chapter 6 he defends an attack against rabbinic *aggadah* by comparing the rabbinic stories to the parables in the New Testament and showing how they are similar. There is no doubt that he could read Martin Luther's translation of the Bible, since he cites how Luther's understanding and translation of certain biblical words agree with his own understanding, in contrast to Brenz's misunderstanding.[19] Zalman Zvi not only relies on Martin Luther to support his argument but also turns for support to the Jewish convert Anthonius[20] Margaritha and his notorious work, *Der Gantz Jüdisch Glaub* (The Whole Jewish Belief [Augsburg, 1530]). Margaritha is cited by name four times.[21] He defends the eating of garlic by Jews against Brenz's

---

17. See the Index of Citations, which lists all the sources cited in the *Theriak*.

18. See the Index of Citations for a full list.

19. *Theriak* 2.26; 5.16.

20. Some primary and secondary sources spell his first name *Anthonius* while others spell it *Antonius*. For consistency I have chosen to use the first form.

21. *Theriak* 2.19; 2.30; 5.4; 5.16. Margaritha's life and work are the subjects of a recent book: Michael T. Walton, *Anthonius Margaritha and the Jewish Faith: Jewish Life and Conversion in Sixteenth-Century Germany* (Detroit, MI: Wayne State University Press, 2012). See also Maria Diemling, "Christliche Ethnographien über Juden und Judentum in der Frühen Neuzeit: Die Konvertiten Victor von Carben und Anthonius Margaritha und ihre Darstellung jüdischen Lebens und jüdischer *Religion*" (PhD diss., University of Vienna, 1999); *idem*, "Anthonius Margaritha on the 'Whole Jewish Faith': A Sixteenth-Century Convert from Judaism and His Depiction of the Jewish Religion," in *Jews, Judaism, and the Reformation in Sixteenth-Century Germany*, ed. Dean Phillip Bell and Stephen G. Burnett (Leiden: Brill, 2006), 303–33; Stephen G. Burnett, "Distorted Mirrors: Antonius Margaritha, Johann Buxtorf and Christian Ethnographies of the Jews," *Sixteenth Century Journal* 25, no. 2 (1994): 275–87. See also the many references to Margaritha in Elisheva Carlebach, *Divided Souls: Converts from Judaism in Germany, 1500–1750* (New Haven, CT: Yale University Press, 2001), index, s.v. Margaritha, Anthonius.

negative aspersions by citing the *Judenschul*, a work by the important Christian Hebraist Johannes Buxtorf.[22] He notes, "Johannes Buxtorf writes why Jews eat garlic in his book, *Judenschul*, p. 290 and p. 340."[23] Buxtorf is not the only Christian Hebraist cited by Zalman Zvi. Defending the legitimacy of Kabbalah and its place in Judaism, he lists a number of Christian scholars who were familiar with Kabbalah and spoke positively about it. They include Don Pico della Mirandola, Cornelius Agrippa of Nettesheim, Paracelsus, and Doctor Johann Reuchlin.[24]

YIDDISH AND GERMAN

A question that jumps out from the discussion of Zalman Zvi's biography was his ability to read and understand books written in German. Why was this ability so very rare among Jews before the eighteenth century and Zalman Zvi's ability such a novelty? The divide between Christians and Jews in Germany with regard to German and Yiddish was in the realm of written works and not in spoken encounters. A Jew and a Christian in early modern Germany would have no significant problem speaking to and understanding each other. As Chone Shmeruk has observed,

> In German-speaking countries it was sufficient to transliterate German works, turning the Latin characters into Hebrew ones, in order to make them accessible to the Yiddish speakers, who did not read Latin characters and identified them with the Christian religion, as the definition of the Latin script as *galkhes* (meaning "priests' script") bears witness to. . . . There is no doubt that Yiddish speakers were able to enjoy these texts since they had no difficulty in understanding them.[25]

---

22. The basic study of Buxtorf is Stephen G. Burnett, *From Christian Hebraism to Jewish Studies: Johannes Buxtorf (1564–1629) and Hebrew Learning in the Seventeenth Century* (Leiden: Brill, 1996).

23. The citation is accurate. The discussion of Jews and garlic is found in the Basel (1603) edition, on the pages cited by Zalman Zvi.

24. *Theriak* 1.11.

25. Chone Shmeruk, "Yiddish Literature Beyond the German-Speaking Area," in *Yiddish in Italia: Manuscripts and Printed Books*, ed. Chava Turniansky and Erika Timm (Milan: Associazione Italiana Amici dell'Universita di Gerusalemme, 2003), 205–6. See also Marion Aptroot, "Writing 'Jewish' not 'German': Functional Writing Styles and the Symbolic Function of Yiddish in Early Modern Ashkenaz," *Leo Baeck Institute Yearbook* 55 (2010): 115–28.

Abundant evidence that Yiddish speakers could understand and appreciate popular German literature is found in the numerous Yiddish reworkings and paraphrases that were based on famous Christian romances and tales of knightly chivalry, popular songs, and other such works. Books like the *Shmuel Bukh* and *Melokhim Bukh*, which were rhymed retellings of the biblical books of Samuel and Kings, were modeled on medieval knightly romances. They were even composed in the same rhyme scheme as the *Niebelungen Lied* and *Dietrich of Bern*, and had explicit instructions to be sung to the same tunes as the German romances. A secular Yiddish work like the *Bovo Bukh* by Elijah Levita was explicitly modeled on a medieval Christian romance, in this case *Sir Bevis of Hampton*.[26] Another interesting example is the close relationship between early modern Yiddish songs in Germany and contemporaneous German songs.[27]

The reason for the Jews' inability to read German books was the Jewish attitude toward the Latin alphabet and what it symbolized. Max Weinreich described this attitude in his history of Yiddish:

> The Jewish alphabet was the attribute of Jewishness; gentiles used *galkhes* (Latin, the language of the priests). The name is to be explained thus: in the Middle Ages the art of writing among non-Jews was almost the exclusive possession of the clerics, and this was done chiefly in Latin. In the Hebrew sources the language of the clerics was once designated neutrally by the name *l(a)tin*, but more frequently "the Christian language," and at times even "the language of impurity." The aversion for the language of the clerics was transferred to their script. In the Middle Ages a *seyfer posl* (a flawed book) was any book in non-Jewish characters. The aversion went so far that up to the Emancipation hardly a Jew knew the non-Jewish alphabet; even in non-Jewish official documents Jews signed their Jewish names in Jewish characters.[28]

Christian Hebraists and missionaries to the Jews from the sixteenth to eighteenth centuries lamented that Jews either could not or would not

26. For a survey of this literature, see Jean Baumgarten, *Introduction to Old Yiddish Literature* (New York: Oxford University Press, 2005), 128–206.
27. See the important study by Diana Matut, *Dichtung und Musik im frühneuzeitlichen Aschkenas*, 2 vols. (Leiden: Brill, 2011).
28. Max Weinreich, *History of the Yiddish Language*, 2 vols. (New Haven, CT: Yale University Press, 2008), vol. 1, p. 185. The notes on pp. A164–167 give many examples of sources supporting this argument.

learn to read the Latin alphabet.[29] Some of them suggested that this was a deliberate Jewish strategy to keep Jews from being influenced by Christian works. Johann Christoph Wagenseil, one of the most important Christian missionaries in Germany at the end of the seventeenth and early eighteenth centuries, observed that Jews were even averse to reading Hebrew books that had Latin translations or anything written from left to right. The solution for Wagenseil and other Christians was to bridge this gap by teaching Christian missionaries the rudiments of reading Yiddish. Christian scholars of Judaism and Christian missionaries saw Yiddish as almost a variant of German, and all that one needed to be able to read Yiddish was to learn the Hebrew alphabet and a few rules for understanding the Yiddish vowel system. Christian Hebraists and missionaries published a whole library of books in Yiddish. They published Jewish books so that missionaries would better understand Judaism and the Jewish approach to the Bible so that they could better comprehend and counter Jewish arguments. Missionaries also published missionary tracts and Yiddish translations of Christian theological works for distribution to Jews to further their missionary efforts.[30] Interesting early examples of this phenomenon are the first two published Yiddish translations of the Jewish liturgical Bible.[31] These were published several months apart in 1544. One edition was published by a Christian Hebraist, Paulus Fagius, in Constance, and the second by a Jewish convert, Paulus Aemilius, in Augsburg.[32]

A related question is why the anti-Jewish literature by converts was a product only of Germany, with the exception of a few works in Italy.[33] The fact that Jews in Germany were not divided by language from their

---

29. Aya Elyada has documented the Christian interest in and attitude toward Yiddish in early modern Germany in her monograph, *A Goy Who Speaks Yiddish: Christians and the Jewish Language in Early Modern Germany* (Stanford, CA: Stanford University Press, 2012).

30. Ibid., 31–32. See also her article, "'Eigentlich Teutsch?' Depictions of Yiddish and Its Relations to German in Early Modern Christian Writings," *European Journal of Jewish Studies* 4, no. 1 (2010): 23–43.

31. The Jewish liturgical Bible contains the *Torah* (Five Books of Moses), the *Haftorot* (sections of the Prophets read in the synagogue as part of the Sabbath service), and the Five Scrolls, which are also read during certain festivals.

32. For a description of these editions and the reasons for their publication, see my article, "The Yiddish *Humash* in the Sixteenth Century," in the forthcoming Ze'ev Gries festschrift (Jerusalem: Carmel, 2016).

33. Carlebach, *Divided Souls*, 173.

Christian neighbors—unlike the case in Eastern Europe—is an additional factor to be considered. The Yiddish spoken by a German Jew was easily comprehensible to a German Christian, but the same could not be said of Yiddish-speaking Eastern European Jews living among Eastern European Christians. Thus, for a German Jewish convert to write a book describing Jewish customs with which he was familiar from his previous life, it would not take much more than learning the Latin alphabet, as most German Jews, men and women, could read and write Yiddish. An editor/printer could relatively easily correct the manuscript's style, grammar, and syntax. This would also explain the extensive repetition of certain themes and ideas found in these works. Converts could read Margaritha or one of the other classics and produce their own works, adding or deleting as they or their Christian mentors thought appropriate.

Zalman Zvi had acquired his facility in the Latin alphabet and wide-ranging knowledge of Christianity as a result of living in foreign lands for many years. Most likely he acquired this ability during his stay in Italy. By the end of the sixteenth century, most Ashkenazi Jews in Italy were no longer using Yiddish as their *lingua franca* but had switched to Italian, as Moses Shulvass observed: "By the second half of the sixteenth century, most of the Ashkenazi Jews too spoke Italian."[34] The taboo against learning or using the Latin alphabet lasted well into the eighteenth century in Germany,[35] but it was never entrenched in Italy, or it disappeared very early.

SAMUEL FRIEDRICH BRENZ

Samuel Friedrich Brenz, as he was known after his conversion, was not especially distinctive as a convert, and his book was not particularly unusual or innovative within the genre of anti-Jewish books by converts from Judaism. To the extent that his book had any notoriety or interest beyond its initial publication, it was always in connection with Zalman Zvi's critique. Some basic facts of Brenz's life and conversion have been preserved, though the sources sometimes disagree about certain dates.

34. Moses Shulvass, *The Jews in the World of the Renaissance* (Leiden: Brill, 1973), 41. More broadly, see *idem*, "Ashkenazim in Italy," in *Between the Rhine and the Bosporus: Studies and Essays in European Jewish History* (Chicago: College of Jewish Studies Press, 1964), 158–83.

35. It is noteworthy that the first Jewish translation of the Torah into High German, Moses Mendelssohn's *Biur*, published in 1783, had to be printed in the Hebrew alphabet for it to have any acceptance in the Jewish community.

Originally named Löw, he was born in Osterberg, near Memmingen, and worked as a Jewish servant of the Count of Oettingen. Löw, his wife, and two sons were baptized in Feuchtwangen, and he received the Christian name Samuel Friedrich Brenz.[36]

Wilhelm Schaudig quotes the following notice in his history of the city of Feuchtwangen:

> Under the Dean Monninger, 1597–1607, who had previously been rector in Ansbach, the Jew Löw, his wife, and two sons were baptized on July 12, 1599. He published the *Jüdischer abgestreiffter Schlangen-Balg*, published in Nürnberg, 1612.[37] He received the name Samuel Friedrich Brenz. His older son, Viktorin Christoph Brenz,[38] was later the pastor in Auernheim, and in 1620, as a student in Feuchtwangen, married Margarete Beck, the daughter of a Christian bürger.[39]

ZALMAN ZVI AND BRENZ

Zalman Zvi mentions in the *Theriak* that there was a personal relationship between him and Brenz that was strongly antagonistic, and it was this relationship that motivated Zalman Zvi to compose his book in the specific form that it had. Zalman Zvi adds some other data about Brenz, though one must keep in mind that this information cannot be verified and that he considered Brenz his enemy. Zalman Zvi tells us that the direct motivation to write the book was a personal encounter with Brenz. He writes in the Introduction:

---

36. This is the information found in an article by Dr. Samuel Maher, "Korrespondenz: Salomon Zebi, der Theriakolog," *Allgemeine Zeitung des Judentums* 23 (1846): 340–42. An entry by S. Mannheimer, "Samuel Friedrich Brenz," is found in the *Jewish Encyclopedia*, vol. 3 (New York: Funk and Wagnalls, 1901–6), 370, but the encyclopedia has no entry for Zalman Zvi of Aufhausen. The *Jewish Encyclopedia* entry is primarily based on the *Allgemeine Zeitung des Judentums* article.

37. This should be 1614.

38. J. F. A. de le Roi, *Die evangelische Christenheit und die Juden*, 3 vols. (Karlsruhe and Leipzig: Reuther, 1884), vol. 1, pp. 123–24, has a short biography of Brenz's older son. He mentions that the Count of Oettingen sponsored his education at the Latin school in Feuchtwangen, and he later became a Protestant pastor in several places.

39. Wilhelm Schaudig, *Geschichte der Stadt und des ehmaligen Stiftes Feuchtwangen* (Feuchtwangen: Sommer & Schorr, 1927), 131–32.

> It [the *Schlangenbalg*] was placed before me, and worthy people waved it under my nose. As a result I called the aforementioned apostate a liar, as I continue to do to the present. On Monday, the seventh of *Ab*, he [Brenz] rode up to my door in a violent manner and threatened me and wanted to kill me. He publicly confirmed the wickedness of his book in front of Jews and Christians, said that it was all true and just, and wanted to continue persecuting Jews. However, I sanctified the name of God in response to his desecration of God's name and called him a liar to his face and swore to write a book against his lies, in a similar form, and to prepare it for publication.[40]

This tells us much about the personal relationship between the two men and Zalman Zvi's motivation for writing his book. A constant theme in the work is Zalman Zvi's demonstration and exposure of Brenz's Jewish ignorance. He shows that when Brenz attempts to cite something in Hebrew, it comes out as gibberish, and he cites many examples of Jewish customs that Brenz did not understand. Zalman Zvi calls him a water carrier and a ropemaker; in other words, a person of no real education.[41] He also cast aspersions on Brenz's character. Zalman Zvi writes that Brenz borrowed many horses that he never returned; if they were all brought together, one would have enough horses to outfit a regiment of cavalry.[42] He adds that Brenz was a usurer while a Jew and continued his usurious practices even after his conversion to Christianity.[43] It is impossible to know if Zalman Zvi's accusations are true. However, the picture he paints of a person who was marginal and possibly alienated from the Jewish community was not an uncommon profile for many of the Jewish converts to Christianity during this period.[44]

Zalman Zvi also writes that he first wrote to the leading rabbis of Germany and Prague, imploring them to defend the Jews and Judaism against Brenz's accusations. He did not receive a suitable response, so he felt the obligation had fallen on his shoulders to make whatever sacrifices were necessary to answer the false accusations against Judaism that were being spread by Brenz.[45]

---

40. *Theriak*, Introduction.
41. *Theriak* 1.7.
42. *Theriak* 1.17.
43. *Theriak* 3.11.
44. The basic study of Jewish converts in the early modern period is Carlebach, *Divided Souls*.
45. *Theriak*, Introduction.

ANTI-JEWISH LITERATURE IN THE EARLY MODERN PERIOD

The *Schlangenbalg* is an example of an anti-Jewish work that took the fear of Jewish blasphemy as its central concern. This was a genre of anti-Jewish literature that first developed in Germany at the beginning of the sixteenth century; it was popular and widespread during the early modern period and well into the eighteenth century. As Elisheva Carlebach has observed:

> The fear of Jewish blasphemy emerged as a central motif in German thinking about Jews around the turn of the sixteenth century. Udo Arnoldi has traced the evolution of the blasphemy threat as the critical factor in the Protestant discussion over the toleration of Jews from Luther through the eighteenth century.[46] It is on this delicate question of tone, then, that accusations of Jewish blasphemy often turned. Whether a Jewish voice uttered a statement of fact or a vile defamation depended on the very subjective judgment of the Christian hearer.[47]

The first part of the sixteenth century saw a significant shift in the centuries-old theological debate between Jews and Christians in Europe. The traditional field of dispute had been the interpretation of the Bible and theology. The disputants on both sides of the debate were important rabbis on the Jewish side and theologians or highly educated Jewish converts on the Christian side, with the field of battle a face-to-face learned disputation, usually before a king or other ruler.[48] The last disputation of this type was between Joseph of Rosheim, leader of the Jewish community in

46. Udo Arnoldi, *Pro Judaeis: Die Gutachten der hallischen Theologen im 18. Jahrhundert zu Fragen der Judentoleranz* (Berlin: Institut Kirche und Judentum, 1993), 26f.

47. Elisheva Carlebach, "Jewish Responses to Christianity in Reformation Germany," in *Jews, Judaism, and the Reformation in Sixteenth-Century Germany*, ed. Dean Phillip Bell and Stephen G. Burnett (Leiden: Brill, 2006), 452.

48. For a survey of the literature and bibliography on the medieval Jewish-Christian polemics, see Kenneth Stow, "The Church and the Jews: From St. Paul to Paul IV," *Bibliographical Essays in Medieval Jewish Studies: The Study of Judaism Volume II* (New York: Ktav, 1976), 109–65; Heinz Schreckenberg, *Die christliche Adversus-Judaeos-Texte und ihr literarisches und historisches Umfeld (1–20 Jh.)*, 3 vols. (Frankfurt am Main: Peter Lang, 1982–94).

the Holy Roman Empire, and the Jewish convert Anthonius Margaritha. This disputation took place on June 25, 1530, at the Imperial Diet of Augsburg, in the presence of the emperor and members of the diet. Joseph of Rosheim was able to convince the emperor and the diet that Margaritha's accusations against the Jews were false.[49]

In place of face-to-face disputations by members of the intellectual elite, two genres of anti-Jewish polemical literature became popular in early modern Germany, beginning early in the sixteenth century and continuing into the eighteenth century. This literature was in the vernacular—that is, German—and many of these works were written by Jewish converts to Christianity.[50] The first genre continued older Christian anti-Jewish accusations of blasphemy and engaging in secret rituals, magical practices, and even witchcraft, which were designed to harm Christians and their belongings.[51] The *Schlangenbalg* is an example of this genre. The second genre, which became the more widespread form of anti-Jewish literature, has been termed "Jewish ceremonial" or "Jewish ethnographic" literature.[52] It was not concerned with the fine points of theology, which had been the focus of the medieval polemics, but instead concentrated on contemporary Jewish rituals and religious practices and their negative influence. Not only did these rituals and practices keep the Jews from seeing the truth of Christianity, but many of them were also magical assaults that negatively affected Christian lives and property.

---

49. On this disputation, see Selma Stern, *Josel of Rosheim: Commander of Jewry in the Holy Roman Empire of the German Nation* (Philadelphia: Jewish Publication Society, 1965), 98–106. Joseph of Rosheim wrote about Margaritha and the disputation in several places in his writings. See Chava Fraenkel-Goldschmidt, *The Historical Writings of Joseph of Rosheim: Leader of Jewry in Early Modern Germany* (Leiden: Brill, 2006), s.v., index, Margaritha, Anthonius.
50. Carlebach, *Divided Souls*, 47–66.
51. For an overview, see Elisheva Carlebach, "Attributions of Secrecy and Perceptions of Jewry," *Jewish Social Studies* 2, no. 3 (1996): 115–36.
52. The most comprehensive study of this literature is Yaacov Deutsch, *Judaism in Christian Eyes: Ethnographic Descriptions of Jews and Judaism in Early Modern Europe* (New York: Oxford University Press, 2012). Deutsch (65–76) lists seventy-eight books on Jewish rituals and ceremonies and nine books containing translations of Jewish prayers. R. Po-Hsia first noted the importance of Christian polemical ethnographies of Jews and Judaism composed by both Christian Hebraists and Jewish converts to Christianity. Other scholars have followed his lead, and this has become an area of scholarly interest in recent years.

Elisheva Carlebach, in her important study of Jewish converts to Christianity in early modern Germany, reviewed earlier explanations for this change and offered her own perspective.[53] Ronald Po-Hsia suggested that the blood libel trial in Trent (1475) was the turning point that sparked the sudden rise in interest in Jewish ritual as opposed to theology. Carlebach correctly points out that blood libels continued in many places and periods, but the interest in Jewish customs and religious practices was a uniquely German phenomenon. She cites Sander Gilman as suggesting that the discrediting of one of the early converts, Johannes Pfefferkorn, and his knowledge of Hebrew by Johannes Reuchlin and other Christian Hebraists led Anthonius Margaritha to create a new field of scholarship for converts to display their knowledge of Judaism. Carlebach herself suggests the importance of *minhag* (religious customs) in Ashkenazi Jewish life as a determining factor. As she writes, "One of the wellsprings of this sphere of literary creativity cultivated by Jewish converts can be found deep within the religious-mental structures of Ashkenaz, the German-Jewish world that the converts had inhabited and left. Emphasis on ritual and *minhag* (custom) formed the core of Ashkenazic culture."[54]

Though there is merit in the suggestions of Gilman and Carlebach, they do not resolve all the issues. Discrediting one ignoramus should not necessarily discredit all converts, as Gilman suggests. Rather, I would suggest another possibility that needs further study. Perhaps this group of converts was not particularly learned in Jewish texts and rabbinic literature. Many of the converts often boasted of their distinguished rabbinic pedigrees. Anthonius Margaritha, for example, was the son and grandson of distinguished rabbis and the brother of the cantor of the Jewish community in Regensburg.[55] These facts are often cited as evidence that he must have been a learned Jew whose comments about Judaism carry the weight and authority of serious learning and knowledge. However, as we will see, patrimony, even when true, is no indicator of actual knowledge. As the New Testament puts it, "You will know them by their fruits."[56] The level of Jewish knowledge these authors demonstrated in their works may be as vital a determinant for their subject matter as the importance of *minhag* in Ashkenazi Jewry. If they had no serious rabbinic education, they could write only about what they knew. These would be the normal practices and customs that every Jew would have been exposed to, in

---

53. Carlebach, *Divided Souls*, 173–77.

54. Ibid., 175.

55. Ibid., 122–23.

56. Matthew 7:16 (NRSV).

contrast to the medieval apostates who could quote abstract concepts, obscure passages, and fine points of biblical grammar. Do any of the early modern converts display a serious knowledge of rabbinic literature or facility with texts that are available only in Hebrew? A detailed study of the level of Jewish knowledge these converts display in their works, in comparison to the level of Jewish knowledge found in contemporaneous Yiddish works, would be helpful in resolving this question. The *Theriak* would also be useful as a comparison text. Zalman Zvi displayed an ability to cite rabbinic texts in their original language and to cite exactly where a Talmudic text was found. Zalman Zvi was not a great rabbi by the standards of his day, but he was "a learned Jew," and his level of erudition would be a good yardstick against which to measure the converts and their claims to rabbinic erudition. It is clear from the evidence of the *Theriak* that Brenz, for example, fails this test. Zalman Zvi gives numerous examples of Brenz's lack of knowledge of Judaism and inability to properly quote Hebrew passages or terms.

It would also appear that the most famous convert of the sixteenth century, Anthonius Margaritha, might also have been less learned than has been assumed. The first modern study of his *Der Gantz Jüdisch Glaub* by a Jewishly knowledgeable scholar was written by Josef Mieses.[57] Maria Diemling's evaluation of Mieses's findings supports suspicions about the level of Margaritha's Jewish knowledge. She writes, "As already (grudgingly) acknowledged by Josef Mieses, Margaritha's book provides some valuable insights into Jewish daily life in early sixteenth-century Ashkenaz, and it is a generally reliable source for established rituals as well as for folk beliefs and liturgical history."[58] Diemling also observes, "Anthonius Margaritha is one of the few converts whose information is generally trusted by later Christian generations, even if it is double-checked by more sophisticated scholars and not always found to be correct."[59] To put it somewhat differently, Margaritha was a Jew, and he knew what the average Jew of his time and place would have known about Jewish life and practice, but the idea that he was some sort of "rabbi" or serious scholar is far from demonstrated.

More conclusive evidence is found in Diemling's summary of Mieses's analysis of Margaritha's translation of the *siddur* (the Jewish

57. *Die älteste gedruckte deutsche Uebersetzung des jüdischen Gebetbuches a. d. Jahre 1530 und ihr Autor Anthonius Margaritha: Eine literarhistorische Untersuchung* (Vienna: R. Löwit, 1916).

58. Diemling, "Anthonius Margaritha on the 'Whole Jewish Faith,'" 312.

59. Ibid., 331 and 331n. 97.

prayerbook): "The greatest part of his translation is dedicated to *Shaharit*, the morning prayers[;] *Minhah* and *Ma'ariv*, in which many of the *Shaharit* prayers are treated much more briefly."[60] She continues:

> The quality of Margaritha's translation was harshly criticized by Josef Mieses, who wrote the first scholarly study of Margaritha's opus. Mieses objected to the Hebrew orthography and the transcription of Hebrew words into German and found more than 40 severe errors in Margaritha's translation. Margaritha was not consistent in Hebrew orthography, and he often wrote Hebrew words phonetically, using a grammatically incorrect *vav* instead of the vowel *kametz*. A more serious problem was the incorrect dividing of sentences, which explains many of his erroneous translations. However, none of his grammatical errors hints at a deliberate distortion of Jewish prayers for polemical reasons. Even if Margaritha's own judgment of his abilities may appear a bit exaggerated,[61] his knowledge of Hebrew was apparently sufficient to teach at the university level.[62]

Margaritha's checkered career as a "university teacher of Hebrew" may partially be explained by his level of knowledge of Hebrew.[63] In contrast to Margaritha, another contemporary Jewish convert, Paulus Aemilius, who had a much better demonstrated knowledge of Hebrew, was appointed a professor of Hebrew at the University of Ingolstadt and managed to keep his position from 1547 until his death in 1575.[64]

JEWISH RESPONSE

Another difference between the medieval polemical literature and the early modern anti-Jewish literature published by converts from Judaism

60. Ibid., 323. The daily prayers and their meanings are what a child would learn in the *heder* (elementary school).

61. Diemling's footnote here reads: "See Anthonius Margaritha, *Erklerung*, Q2v [=62v], where he states that Jews know less Hebrew grammar than a Christian pupil who has studied with him or another teacher for only a year."

62. Diemling, "Anthonius Margaritha on the 'Whole Jewish Faith,'" 323.

63. On his teaching career, see ibid., 306–7.

64. On Aemilius, see my article, "Paulus Aemilius, Convert to Catholicism and Printer of Yiddish Books in Sixteenth-Century Augsburg," *Judaica: Beiträge zum Verstehen des Judentums* 71, no. 4 (2015): 349–65.

is the lack of a public Jewish response to these works. There are no Jewish published responses to the anti-Jewish literature produced by the converts, with the one exception of the *Yudisher Theriak*.[65] Several possible reasons present themselves. The Jews were not forced to respond by the authorities, as they had been in the medieval period, and this literature was aimed at a Christian audience and published in an alphabet most Jews could not or would not read. In addition there is no evidence that these works directly affected the Jews adversely. Many of the accusations, like those that Jews used magic against Christians, were already part of general Christian folklore. It is uncertain whether these books created or significantly contributed to the spread of these ideas among the ordinary Christian populace. Rather, the primary audience for these works was probably Christian clergy and officials. They may also have served as a form of self-advertisement for the authors to obtain employment or financial support. Many of the converts tried to compete with the Christian Hebraists as experts in Hebrew and/or Judaism on the strength of their books. The career of Anthonius Margaritha is a good example of this phenomenon.[66]

CONTENTS OF THE *THERIAK*

The *Theriak* is a direct response to the *Schlangenbalg*. Therefore its organization and contents are dictated by the form and contents of the *Schlangenbalg*. Zalman Zvi provides a detailed "List of the Apostate's Accusations" at the end of his work. He lists each chapter and provides a brief description of the theme of each paragraph within each chapter. The description summarizes the accusation against the Jews made in the *Schlangenbalg*. Though each chapter has a major theme, there are many miscellaneous issues mentioned, particularly toward the end of a given chapter. Thus one must look through the whole list of subjects if one is interested in a specific theme.

The first chapter focuses on Jesus and the Jewish attitude toward him. Some sections are derived from Talmudic traditions and stories that portray Jesus in a negative light. Other paragraphs describe how Jews talk about Jesus in a mocking manner and make him an object of ridicule.

65. For a bibliography of Jewish anti-Christian polemical works, see Judah Rosenthal, "Anti-Christian Polemical Literature" [Hebrew], *Areshet* 2 (1960): 130–79; 3 (1961): 433–39. The *Theriak* is the only postmedieval work listed in this bibliography.

66. On Margaritha's life and career, see the sources cited earlier, in notes 21 and 57.

The second chapter is a response to Brenz's accusations about how the Jews mock and speak disrespectfully about the Catholic and Protestant churches and clergy. Jews were also accused of mocking Christian rituals and practices such as undergoing baptism, wearing church vestments, ringing church bells, receiving the Eucharist, and others.

The third through fifth chapters contain responses to more than seventy-five accusations against Jews about how they hate, denigrate, curse, and mock Christians in all aspects of their lives: Jews curse Christians in their daily interactions; they have no respect for Christian religious and civil institutions; they permit lying to and cheating of Christians in business and even boast about it to each other; they pray for the destruction of Christian kingdoms and call them "kingdoms of wickedness." These accusations are repeated in many variations.

The sixth chapter is devoted to demonstrating Brenz's ignorance of rabbinic literature. Zalman Zvi tries to show that Brenz's citations are based on complete ignorance and should not be considered seriously. He goes further and shows that Brenz not only did not know rabbinic literature but also did not know the Christian Gospels. In contrast Zalman Zvi demonstrates his own knowledge of the Gospels and speaks positively about the stories and parables that are found in the New Testament.

The last chapter, the seventh, is devoted to the subject of the Messiah. Zalman Zvi explains how the Talmudic sages understood the concept and again emphasizes that Brenz lied about it and did not know anything about the subject.

SOURCES OF THE *THERIAK*

Zalman Zvi uses a wide variety of sources in his polemic against Brenz's accusations. The Jewish sources encompass the whole gamut, including biblical verses, Talmudic and Midrashic sources, and a number of medieval authorities.[67] Much less expected are the Christian sources that are cited by Zalman Zvi, especially the New Testament. Even more surprising is the number and variety of these citations.[68] He also quotes Christian Hebraists and even Jewish converts like Anthonius Margaritha when it supports his argument against Brenz. Though many medieval Jewish scholars could cite Christian sources in their polemics, Jews in early

67. The Index of Citations at the end of this volume gives a detailed list of all Jewish sources cited and provides the location of the citation in the text.

68. The Index of Citations at the end of this volume gives a detailed list of all New Testament verses cited and provides the location of the citation in the text.

modern Germany were discouraged from learning the Latin alphabet and reading German texts.[69] This attitude was very different from that which prevailed in Italy, where Jews regularly read and wrote in Italian by the beginning of the seventeenth century.

The author who influenced Zalman Zvi perhaps more than any other was Josephus. He tells us that it was Josephus's *Against Apion* that inspired him to respond to Brenz using the form he adopted in the *Theriak*.[70] He cites Josephus at least fourteen times, usually as providing an example for how to respond to attacks on Jews and Judaism.[71] At first glance this should not be surprising. A Hebrew epitome of Josephus's writings was composed between the tenth and eleventh centuries and became known as *Sefer Yosippon* (The Book of Yosippon). *Yosippon* was the name by which the author (Josephus) was known in Jewish literature, and how Zalman Zvi cited him. The book was an important source for Jewish writers of historical chronicles in the medieval and early modern periods when they wrote about the history of the Second Temple period and the events surrounding the Temple's destruction.[72] The *Sefer Yosippon* was also one of the earliest Jewish books printed, and four Hebrew editions had been produced by the time Zalman Zvi wrote the *Theriak*.[73] The *Sefer Yosippon* was also translated into Yiddish and printed in Zurich in 1546.[74] In addition, a Hebrew translation of Josephus's work, *Contra Apion*, was published as an appendix in Abraham Zacuto's *Sefer Yuhasin*.[75] A comparison of Zacuto's Hebrew translation of *Contra Apion* with the original seems to indicate that it contains the complete text. Thus it is possible that this edition could have served as Zalman Zvi's source for his discussion of *Contra Apion*. It is also possible that he had access to a German edition of Josephus's writings.

---

69. See note 28 in this introduction.

70. *Theriak*, Introduction.

71. *Theriak* 1.7; 1.13; 3.1.7; 3.1.9; 3.1.13–3.1.16; 3.12; 4.25. Several sections reference multiple citations in one paragraph.

72. The most comprehensive introduction to the work and its historical significance is David Flusser, *Sefer Yosippon*, vol. 2 (Jerusalem: Bialik Institute, 1980), 3–252.

73. See Moritz Steinschneider, *Catalogus Librorum Hebraeorum in Bibliotheca Bodleiana* (Berlin: Friedlander, 1852–60), no. 6033. There are two modern scholarly editions of this text. The text of the standard edition that was reprinted over the centuries is found in Hayyim Hominer, *Sefer Yosippon*, 4th ed. (Jerusalem: Hominer Publishing, 1978). Flusser's edition (see previous note) was based on a different manuscript.

74. On the Yiddish translation of *Sefer Yosippon*, see Nochem Shtif, "Michael Adam's Three Yiddish Books" [Yiddish], *Filologishe Shriftn* 2 (1928): 135–68.

At the same time, a careful examination of Zalman Zvi's Josephus citations in comparison to the *Sefer Yosippon* shows that Zalman Zvi was not quoting the *Sefer Yosippon* but must have been using a more complete, non-Jewish edition of Josephus. References to "Book," "Romans," and chapter numbers, for example, are not found in any edition of the *Sefer Yosippon.*[76] The complete works of Josephus were not known in Jewish sources until the second half of the sixteenth century. The first Jewish author to discuss Josephus in terms of his original writings was Azariah de'Rossi, in his innovative historical work *The Light of the Eyes* (*Meor Eynai'im*), first published in Mantua, in 1573.[77] His work was very controversial in his lifetime, and it was scorned by his contemporaries. It was only in the nineteenth century that his writings were rediscovered, and he came to be seen as the father of modern Jewish historiography.[78] It is unlikely that Zalman Zvi would have been familiar with de' Rossi and his work, and there is no evidence in the *Theriak* that would make this connection.

Since, as we have seen, Zalman Zvi could read German, the likeliest possibility would be that he used a German edition of Josephus's writings as his source of knowledge about Josephus. There were a large number of editions of Josephus's writings before 1615, in a number of languages, so it is impossible to determine which edition Zalman Zvi utilized, beyond the assertion that his knowledge of Josephus came from editions other than the *Sefer Yosippon.*[79]

---

75. First published in Constantinople, 1561 (Steinschneider, *Catalogus*, no. 4303, 2). It was reprinted in Cracow, 1581. However, the *Contra Apion* appendix was deleted in this edition, and a different text was substituted in its place (Steinschneider, *Catalogus*, no. 4303, 3). The modern scholarly edition is *Sefer Yuhasin ha-Shalem,* ed. Herschell Filipowski (London, 1857). A second edition of *Sefer Yuhasin ha-Shalem* was published with a new introduction by Abraham H. Freimann (Frankfurt am Main: Wahrmann, 1924).

76. The passages from Josephus cited in the *Theriak* can be found in Appendix 2.

77. The second printing of this work was published in Berlin (1794). The modern scholarly edition and translation into English was published as Azariah de'Rossi, *The Light of the Eyes*, ed. and trans. Joanna Weinberg (New Haven, CT: Yale University Press, 2001).

78. On de'Rossi and his work, see Salo Baron, *History and Jewish Historians* (Philadelphia: Jewish Publication Society of America, 1964), 167–239.

79. The most complete bibliography of early editions of Josephus's work is Heinz Schreckenberg, *Bibliographie zu Flavius Josephus* (Leiden: Brill, 1968). For the editions before 1615, see pp. 1–21. It is noteworthy that the editions of the *Sefer Yosippon* are not included in this bibliography.

POLEMICAL STRATEGY

Zalman Zvi adopted a multipronged strategy in his attack on the *Schlangenbalg* and its author. His goal was to discredit Brenz as an ignoramus who was completely unreliable as an expert on Jews and Judaism. At the same time he also had an apologetic goal: to defend Jews and Judaism against broader accusations that were more widespread and which were found in many Christian works that attacked Jews and Judaism. He never lost an opportunity to demonstrate Brenz's ignorance of Hebrew, the Hebrew Bible, and even the New Testament. When Brenz attacked the stories found in the Talmud, Zalman Zvi responded that Brenz did not even know his own scriptures. He then went on to cite a number of parables and stories from the New Testament that he compared to the rabbinic *aggadot* (stories and legends), and he demonstrates their similarities.[80]

Not only did Zalman Zvi quote the New Testament against Brenz, but he also cited Christian authorities. For instance, Zalman Zvi cited Martin Luther's translation of the Bible to show that Luther agreed with his interpretation of the word *goy*, which could mean either gentile or nation, including the Jews, depending on the context.[81] Even the convert Anthonius Margaritha, the author of one of the most influential Christian ethnographic works, is quoted as an authority against Brenz.[82] When Brenz attacked Kabbalah, Zalman Zvi observed that there were famous Christian scholars, whom he mentioned by name, who were devotees of Kabbalah.[83]

Zalman Zvi also used daily reality to show that Brenz was spreading falsehoods. For example, Brenz argued that when Jews passed through a city, they cursed the city and all the produce found in that city's markets. Zalman Zvi easily pointed out how nonsensical this was. Since Jews were not allowed to engage in agriculture, they had to rely on Christians for their foodstuffs. Why would they curse the very food they needed for their own sustenance?[84] Similarly, in response to Brenz's claim that "Jewish physicians consider it a positive commandment to kill Christians," Zalman Zvi appealed to everyday reality. It was well known that Jewish physicians were held in high esteem and consulted in all world centers. This conclusion was so self-evident that it did not even need explicit

---

80. *Theriak* 6.1.

81. *Theriak* 5.16.

82. *Theriak* 2.19; 2.30; 5.4; 5.16.

83. *Theriak* 1.11.

84. *Theriak* 4.16.

mention.[85] John Efron, in his study of Christian antipathy toward Jewish physicians, shows that the lies about them were widespread, but this did not stop Christians of all social classes from availing themselves of the services of Jewish physicians. Brenz's attack was a typical example of the antipathy that was found in much of the anti-Jewish literature from the Middle Ages through the early modern period.[86]

Another category of apologetic relates to popular beliefs about Jews that cannot be dismissed by appeals to logic or demonstrations of Brenz's general ignorance, including knowledge of Hebrew and Jewish practice and even his ignorance of the New Testament. These were accusations and concepts that were generally widespread in all sectors of the Christian community. They were matters of faith and belief, as opposed to things that were objectively demonstrable or provable. Some of these included beliefs and traditions about Jesus, Jewish practices on Christmas Eve, and the custom of eating garlic. The Jewish relationship to magic, and its nefarious use by Jews against Christians, is also a theme that is found in the *Theriak*.

Zalman Zvi's apologetic method in his approach to the central question of the Jewish relationship with Jesus was to adopt what might be called "the two Jesuses theory." He argued that the negative rabbinic stories about Jesus actually referred to a disciple of Rabbi Joshua ben Perahia, who lived more than a hundred years before the historical Yeshua of Nazareth, who was the founder of Christianity. He was careful to call the "bad" Jesus "Yeshu," while the "good" Jesus was called "Yeshua."[87] He also referred to the "good" Jesus as "Yeshua of Nazareth." All the negative references cited by Brenz—which he claimed to have found in rabbinic literature and later Jewish sources about Jesus and his disciples—referred to the "bad" Jesus, Yeshu, and not to Yeshua of Nazareth. Another strategy Zalman Zvi used here was to clarify the meanings of the words *tola* and *taluy* (hanged). He cites a number of biblical verses to show that *tola* means "scarlet" and not "hanged," while *taluy* means "uncertain" and refers to a sacrifice that was offered in the Temple.[88] He resorts to a

85. *Theriak* 4:22.

86. John M. Efron, "Interminably Maligned: The Conventional Lies about Jewish Doctors," in *Jewish History and Jewish Memory: Essays in Memory of Yosef Hayim Yerushalmi*, ed. Elisheva Carlebach, John M. Efron, and David N. Myers (Hanover, NH: Brandeis University Press, 1998), 301, 309, nn. 28 and 29.

87. *Jesus* or *Jesu* is the Greek version of the name; *Yeshua* is the proper Hebrew name.

88. *Theriak* 1.1–2.

variety of similar strategies to respond to and deflect the various accusations made by Brenz.

The source of most of the negative stories about Jesus that Brenz and other converts used in their polemics was a work called *Toledot Yeshu*. Brenz refers to this work under another name, *Ma'aseh Tola* (Story of the Hanged One). This work was quietly circulated in manuscript, and Jews, when asked about it, usually denied its existence, as did Zalman Zvi. He said, "I say about this that in all my life I have never seen such a book. I wonder, if this book was a secret, where did the apostate see it?"[89] It was also a work of great interest to Christian Hebraists. Several Christian Hebraists mentioned having seen a manuscript of *Toledot Yeshu*, but a full edition was first published by Johann Christoph Wagenseil only in 1681.[90] Prior to this publication, it was clandestinely circulated in manuscript and was the subject of much speculation regarding its contents and significance.[91]

Another issue that was controversial and the subject of interest among Christian Hebraists was the Jewish affinity for garlic.[92] The Jewish association with garlic is already found in the Bible,[93] and it continued through the Talmudic period and into the medieval period. With the advent of the printing press and the rediscovery of the medical theories of Galen, garlic fell into disfavor among the elite classes of Christian society in

89. *Theriak* 1.7.

90. It was included in Wagenseil's *Tela ignea Satanae* (Flaming Arrows of Satan [Altdorf, 1681]). The modern scholarly edition is Michael Meerson and Peter Schäfer, eds. and trans., *Toledot Yeshu: The Life Story of Jesus* (Tübingen: Mohr Siebeck, 2014). An important collection of studies about the *Toledot Yeshu* is Yaacov Deutsch, Michael Meerson, and Peter Schäfer, eds. *Toledot Yeshu (The Life Story of Jesus) Revisited: A Princeton Conference* (Tübingen: Mohr Siebeck, 2011).

91. Extracts or quotations were published before Wagenseil's edition, such as a piece published by Pocheto Salvaticus in 1520, taken from Raymundo Martini's *Pugio Fidei*. This was also probably the source of the citations by Martin Luther. See Debra Kaplan, *Beyond Expulsion: Jews, Christians, and Reformation Strasbourg* (Stanford, CA: Stanford University Press, 2011), 206, n. 34.

92. A comprehensive study of the role of garlic and its relation to Jews in early modern Germany is Maria Diemling, "'As the Jews Like to Eat Garlick': Garlic in Jewish-Christian Polemical Discourse in Early Modern Germany," in *Food and Judaism: Studies in Jewish Civilization*, vol. 15, ed. Leonard Greenspoon, Ronald Simkins, and Gerald Shapiro (Omaha, NE: Creighton University Press, 2005), 215–34.

93. Numbers 11:5.

the German-speaking lands. The Jews, more influenced by the positive Talmudic references to garlic and less influenced by trends in Christian society, continued to see garlic in a positive light. By the seventeenth century, Johannes Buxtorf, the important Christian Hebraist, connected garlic to anti-Christian sentiments.[94] Zalman Zvi offers responses from a wide variety of sources and a diversity of arguments. First he justifies eating garlic by citing the biblical verses. Being aware of the Christian distaste for garlic, he suggests that Jews eat it at times when they know they will not be in contact with Christians, such as during Christmas. Another argument was that garlic is in fact healthy, contrary to Christian opinion. He then moves on to citing Johannes Buxtorf's important work *Judenschul* (*Synagoga Judaica*) to explain why Jews eat garlic. Finally, he points out that in other countries, like France and Italy, even the highest nobility, not only the masses, eat garlic.[95] The massing of proofs for his argument from a diverse number of sources is a strategy that is often found in the *Theriak*.

Brenz takes his critique about garlic a step further and connects it to Christmas Eve and the desire to mock Jesus and Christianity. He also argues that Jews eat and drink to excess and make merry on Christmas Eve.[96] Zalman Zvi responds that Jews' eating and drinking during this time has nothing to do with Christmas. Rather, their celebrations have to do with the Jewish holiday of Hanukkah, which is a time of rejoicing and family togetherness that often coincides with the Christmas season. He also reminds the reader that the Christmas season was a time of assaults on the Jewish community, thus Jews refrained from interactions with their Christian neighbors around the holiday. There are several accusations made by Brenz that Zalman Zvi ignores. One of them is the idea that the Jews made Jesus crawl through the latrines on Christmas Eve. Referred to as "Nittel Nacht"[97] in Jewish sources, Christmas Eve was characterized by unusual practices and prohibitions among Jews in Central and Eastern Europe.[98] Any attempt by Zalman Zvi to acknowledge

94. Diemling, "As the Jews Like to Eat Garlick," 222.

95. *Theriak* 1.20.

96. Ibid.

97. The most common explanation for the term *Nittel* is that it comes from *Natale* (birth), thus "Nittel Nacht" would be the night of the birth of Jesus.

98. Christmas Eve has historically been problematic for Jews for much of Jewish history. An important study is Marc Shapiro, "Torah Study on Christmas Eve," *Journal of Jewish Thought and Philosophy* 8 (1999): 319–53. Regarding Brenz and the *Theriak*, see especially pp. 340–43. See also Rebecca Scharbach, "The Ghost in the Privy: On the Origins of Nittel Nacht and Modes of Cultural Exchange," *Jewish Studies Quarterly* 20 (2013): 340–73.

such ideas would be too inflammatory, and no defense would be effective. Thus he passes over it in silence, no doubt hoping that other readers would not notice.

The use and misuse of magic and sorcery to harm Christians are additional accusations Brenz throws at the Jews. Here too Zalman Zvi deploys many of his usual strategies. He cites Christian scholars who wrote that Kabbalah was a divine wisdom and not a magical invocation of demonic names. Sorcery was forbidden in the Bible and in the Talmud, so Jews do not engage in it. When Brenz cites a story that Jews raise the Queen of Sheba and other women through necromancy to have sexual relations with them, Zalman Zvi mocks the very idea. What is interesting about this rather bizarre-sounding story is that it has a historical basis. Juspa Shamash of Worms (1604–78), in his book of stories about legends relating to the Jewish community of Worms, *Ma'aseh Nissim*, described precisely such a story; in it, a Jew in Worms had a romantic relationship with the Queen of Sheba, who appeared to him through magical means.[99] Zalman Zvi's mockery can be seen as a form of dissimulation in this instance. Similarly, Zalman Zvi partially dissimulates when he mocks the idea of the golem[100]—that one can take a lump of earth and form it into a person, whisper certain incantations over it, and bring it to life. He admits that the Talmud discusses this idea, and ancient kabbalists might have been able to create such beings, but this knowledge is now concealed, and the only golems in his day come from the womb.[101]

In summary, Zalman Zvi's goal was to defuse and refute Brenz's accusations and demonstrate that Brenz was an ignoramus who could not be believed. He utilized a variety of strategies, and appealed to a variety of forms of authority, depending on the accusation and the tools available to him. Mockery and demonstrating Brenz's ignorance—even ignorance of Christian texts like the New Testament—were his primary approaches. Zalman Zvi also cited evidence from Jewish and Christian sources, and did not hesitate to cite both types of sources to buttress a particular argument. He always had two audiences in mind, both Jews and Christians. Thus while a Jewish audience would not be impressed with a citation

99. Juspa Shamash, *Ma'aseh Nissim* (Amsterdam, 1696), story no. 21. Juspa collected these stories in the middle of the seventeenth century, so it is likely they were known at the beginning of that century.

100. The history of this concept is found in Gershom Scholem, "The Idea of the Golem," in *On the Kabbalah and Its Symbolism* (New York: Schocken, 1965), 158–204.

101. *Theriak* 1.11–13.

from the New Testament, such references would get the attention of a Christian audience. Similarly, references to rabbinic sources would be intended for the Jewish readers but not for the Christians. At the same time some of his humorous and mocking comments might get a laugh from both Jews and Christians.

IMPORTANCE OF THE *THERIAK*

The *Yudisher Theriak* is particularly important because it is a unique work. It is the only known early modern Jewish response to the many German-language works published (by Jewish converts to Christianity and Christian Hebraists) in Germany from the sixteenth to the eighteenth century that opposed Judaism and Jews. It offers insights into how Jews might have responded to the widespread accusations they heard in their conversations or other encounters with Christians in Germany. Though there were other defenses of Judaism in early modern Italy, Rabbi Leon Modena's *Historia de' riti hebraici* being the most famous,[102] I would suggest that the social and cultural conditions were so different in Italy that it would be erroneous to compare these works to the *Theriak*. The cultural and religious contexts were entirely different. Italy was a Catholic land, and many of the issues that affected Jews as a result of the Protestant-Catholic confrontation in Germany did not affect Italian Jews. The fact that Modena could publish his work in Italian while Zalman Zvi could not publish his work in German provides eloquent testimony to the differences in the two societies.

A more fruitful comparison that would help us understand the realities of Jewish-Christian relations in early modern Germany would be one that analyzed the arguments of Brenz and the responses of Zalman Zvi as examples of the Jewish-Christian polemic in the seventeenth century. However this would require a significant monograph and a team of scholars with expertise in various specialties, which is beyond the limits

102. On Modena and his *Historia de' riti hebraici*, see Mark R. Cohen, "Leone da Modena's *Riti*: A Seventeenth-Century Plea for Social Toleration of Jews," *Jewish Social Studies* 34 (1972): 287–321. On Modena and his life, see *The Autobiography of a Seventeenth-Century Venetian Rabbi*, ed. and trans. Mark R. Cohen (Princeton, NJ: Princeton University Press, 1988). There were other Italian works in this genre. A somewhat later example is David Malkiel, "The Jewish-Christian Debate on the Eve of Modernity: Joshua Segre of Scandiano and His *Asham Talui*," *Revue des Etudes juives* 164, nos. 1–2 (2005): 157–86.

of this introduction. Johann Wülfer attempted to do something of this sort in his *Theriaca Judaica ad Examen Revocata* in Nürnberg (1681), but his intent was polemical and slanted toward refuting Zalman Zvi's arguments.[103] Johann Eisenmenger's *Endecktes Judentum*, published in 1711,[104] also attempted something similar to Wülfer's work but on a broader scale. An added benefit of such a project would be that, once fact was separated from fantasy, one could glean interesting insights into popular culture among both Jews and Christians of this period.

PUBLICATION HISTORY OF THE *THERIAK*

As mentioned earlier, the *Yudisher Theriak* was first published in Hanau in 1615 as a response to Brenz's *Schlangenbalg*, which was first published in 1614 in Nürnberg and Augsburg.[105] The Nürnberg edition is the best-known version and the one usually cited in the scholarly literature. I have not seen the Augsburg edition cited in the scholarly literature on the *Schlangenbalg*, but I came across it serendipitously while checking the digital book collection of the Bavarian State Library in Munich.

Zalman Zvi's knowledge of the Latin alphabet and his ability to read German led him to attempt something very unusual. He wanted to publish a second version of the *Theriak* in German. He states throughout the *Theriak* that he had prepared another version of the book. One version, written in Yiddish, was intended for a Jewish audience so that Jews should know how to respond to the calumnies against Judaism they might hear from Christians. He wanted to publish another version for Christians in German so that they might have a more positive view of Jews and Judaism.[106] The version for Christians was never published. Many of the questions relating to why the Yiddish edition was published and the German edition of the *Theriak* was not were answered by

103. On his work, see Appendix 1.

104. The book had a complicated publication history. It was first printed in Frankfurt in 1700, but influential members of the Jewish community stopped its publication. Ten years later, King Frederick I of Prussia had it printed in Berlin, but the title page place of printing was changed to Königsberg. Jacob Katz, *From Prejudice to Destruction: Anti-Semitism, 1700–1933* (Cambridge, MA: Harvard University Press, 1980), 13–22, discusses Eisenmenger and his later influence.

105. Appendix 1 contains full bibliographical information for all the editions of the *Schlangenbalg* and *Theriak* discussed here.

106. *Theriak*, Introduction; 7.1.

a group of documents found in Hanau by Prof. Stephen Burnett. He described and analyzed them in his article on the censorship of Hebrew books in Hanau.[107]

Walter Keuchen was the censor of Hebrew books for the press in Hanau. After 1613 he wrote detailed reports about only three books that were potentially controversial.[108] Fortunately for us, the *Theriak* was one of them. The documents relating to his report include a petition by Zalman Zvi requesting permission to publish both the Yiddish and German versions of his book. They also include the reasons why the printing of the Yiddish text was allowed but the German version was forbidden.

The magistrate in Hanau ordered the censor to read both the *Schlangenbalg* and the *Theriak* so that he could pass proper judgment on Zalman's Zvi's book. Keuchen decided that the Yiddish version of the *Theriak* could be printed because it was only a defense of Judaism and in no way an attack on Christianity. Zalman Zvi had been very careful in this regard. He only corrected factual errors in Brenz's quotation of Talmudic passages and biblical verses. For example, in the sixth and seventh chapters of the *Schlangenbalg*, which discuss the concepts of the Messiah and the Trinity, Zalman Zvi studiously avoided engaging any of the theological aspects of these concepts.

Keuchen was enthusiastic about publishing the *Theriak* for a reason that was never intended by Zalman Zvi—one that further explains why the Yiddish edition was published but permission was denied for the German volume. The work would be useful to Christian Hebraists and help them formulate counter arguments to the Jewish objections raised by Zalman Zvi against the missionary works that were being produced with the intention of convincing Jews to convert to Christianity. The Yiddish edition posed no real danger for Christians, since the only Christians who could read the text were a small group of scholars. On the other hand, a German edition would be readily accessible to ordinary Christians and could become an obstacle to their faith.[109]

The fates of the *Theriak* and the *Schlangenbalg* were intertwined for the rest of the seventeenth century. Both works were reprinted in 1680. The *Theriak* reprint was published in Altdorf, a university town near

107. Stephen Burnett, "Hebrew Censorship in Hanau: A Mirror of Jewish-Christian Coexistence in Seventeenth-Century Germany," in *The Expulsion of the Jews: 1492 and After*, ed. Raymond B. Waddington and Arthur H. Williamson (New York: Garland Publishing Inc., 1994), 199–222.

108. Ibid., 206.

109. Burnett, "Hebrew Censorship in Hanau," 208–9.

Nürnberg, and the *Schlangenbalg* in Nürnberg. Both were exact copies of their first editions.[110] No additional information, beyond the names of the printers, was provided about who published these editions or why. The following year a Christian Hebraist did indeed utilize the *Theriak* in the manner envisioned by Walter Keuchen, the Hanau censor of Hebrew books. Johann Wülfer published his *Theriaca Judaica ad Examen Revocata* (1681) in Nürnberg. This work contained a copy of the *Schlangenbalg*, a copy of the *Theriak*, and Wülfer's three-hundred-page commentary analyzing the two works, along with his own judgments. The *Schlangenbalg* and *Theriak* were printed in their respective original languages, German and Yiddish, and appear to be exact reproductions of their respective 1680 editions, maintaining pagination, typeface, and page layout. Wülfer's Latin commentary was written from the perspective of a Christian Hebraist and missionary who sought to explain why Zalman Zvi was wrong and Brenz correct. It has never been properly analyzed, though it might well yield some interesting insights.[111]

The second Christian scholar to utilize the *Theriak* in the same manner was Johann Andreas Eisenmenger in his major work, *Entdecktes Judenthum*. Among the many sources that Eisenmenger utilized were both the *Schlangenbalg* and the *Theriak*. His normal procedure was to cite the *Schlangenbalg* with approval and then attempt to refute the *Theriak*'s critique of the *Schlangenbalg*. Eisenmenger's work has more than thirty references to Zalman Zvi and the *Theriak*, several of them covering multiple pages.[112] This was a common style utilized by many Christian Hebraists from the fifteenth to eighteenth centuries in their studies of Jewish religious texts. Their goal was twofold: to refute the Jewish claims and to prove the superiority or theological correctness of their Christian denomination, whether Lutheran or Calvinist. The ultimate goal was to develop arguments and other tools that would aid Christian missionaries in their work of converting the Jews. This was a Protestant enterprise for the most part. There are no Catholic works commenting on or refuting the *Theriak*.

110. The *Schlangenbalg* had minor variations in orthography on the title page. See Appendix 1.

111. Max Grünbaum, *Jüdischdeutsche Chrestomathie* (Leipzig: Brockhaus, 1882), 560–85, has a sampling of extracts from the *Theriak*. He cites a few comments taken from Wülfer's work, along with his own comments and notes.

112. The page references to Zalman Zvi can be found in the index to volume 1 of *Entdecktes Judenthum* (Konigsberg, 1711), 982. The entry is under "Zalman Zvi, der Rabbi."

Christian interest in the *Theriak* declined by the middle of the eighteenth century. However the *Theriak* was not completely forgotten, and a Jewish work based on it was published in Amsterdam, in 1737, titled *Sefer ha-Nizzahon ha-Nikra Zarei ha-Yehudim* (Book of Victory, That Is Called a Balm for the Jews). It was written in Yiddish and edited by Eliezer Sussman ben Isaac Rödelsheim. It is more of a paraphrase than a translation of the *Theriak*, updating some of the vocabulary but also deleting some things. Eliezer Sussman writes in his introduction that the *Theriak* had become very rare, and that is what motivated him to publish this new edition. A copy is found in the Mehlman Collection of rare Jewish books at the National Library of Israel.[113] One interesting note about this edition is that the editor explains on the title page that the work was published in a small format so that one could keep it in a pocket as a handy reference for refuting Christian arguments.

More than a century later, a Hebrew paraphrase of the *Theriak* was published in Warsaw, in 1873. The connection between this edition and the Amsterdam edition still needs clarification. J. D. Eisenstein republished part of this Hebrew paraphrase in his Hebrew anthology of Jewish apologetic works, *Ozar Vikukhim*, under the title "The Polemic of Rabbi Zalman Zvi Aufhausen Against the Apostate Friedrich Brenz."[114]

113. Isaac Yudlov, *Ginzei Yisrael* (Jerusalem: Jewish National and University Library, 1985), no. 1228.

114. *Ozar Vikukhim* (New York, 1928), 170–84.

אלבין גיוועזין׳ דרום הב איך מיינר קאפיטל אב גיטיילט׳ אונ׳ איקליכן ענין מיט סימנים א׳ ב׳ ג׳ גיצייכנט׳ דא מיט ווען המותר אייבן ענין ברענגט׳ דען ער ואר אויך גשריבן היט׳ אונ׳ ורענטוורט איז׳ אלזו שרייב איך׳ דיא אוש אין דעם קאפיטל אין דעם סימן ורענטוורט זא קאנטו דש זעלביג מיט וויניג מיה אונ׳ ארבייט ויכדן׳ אלזא האב איך אויך אלי פסוקים מאמרים אונ׳ פוסקים מיט מראה מקום ואר צייכנט׳ דעמין נעם ולייסיג אכט:

בשם האל לבבות חוקר׳ אכחישה דובר שקר׳ מזולל אוציא יקר׳

א דש מיר הנוצרים ומשיחם כיט מגנה זיין זולן׳

דרש דאש חכמינו ז״ל׳ כאך קיין ספר ארלויבט אודר הייסט׳ די קריסטן די דא גלויבין אן ישוע נוצרי׳ צו ורארכטן אודר צו ואר שפוטין׳ וויל וויניגר צו זלוכין׳ מיט ווארטן אודר ווערקן צו בילייריגן׳ זינט מולן מיר וואן גאט דעם הערן אונזרי גרוסן עבירות הלבין אוש אונזרם הייליגן לאנד ורטריבן דש בית המקדש ורשטערט׳ אונ׳ אונטר אלי ואלקר גשטריאט אונ׳ אוש גיטיילט זיין׳ זוא אונש דן משה רבינו ע״ה אונ׳ אלי נביאים ואר גיזאגט האבין:

נון האבן די קריסטן דש רעגימענט ואן השי״ת אונ׳ דש זיא בילכר וויא אובר אונש הערשן׳ וויא דן אונזרי חכמים שרייבן׳ דש מיר נוהג כבוד במלכות זיין זולן׳ דש איז דש מיר קייזר קוניג ירשטן אונ׳ הערן אלי גיהורזאם אונ׳ עהר ארווייזן זולן׳ וויא ווייטלעפיג אין זיינם אורט זול בשריבן ווערדן׳ וויא זולטן מיר דען דיא קריסטן איר רעגימענט אודר אמונה ורארכטן׳ דער זולכש טוט׳ דער ורארכטט גאט דען הערן דער די רעגימענט אויס טיילט:

קריסטן קענין דען יודן אך כיט א׳ בלס טון דען זיא האנדלין ווידר אירן מצות׳ ישוע נוצרי וויל כיט דש מאן יודן בוז טון זול׳ זאגט זיא זיין שוגגים אן זיינר מיתה׳

דיא קענין די קריסטן אויך כיט ורארכטווערטן אודר אין אירם גלויבן ווידן אונש יודן צו בישעדיגן אודר צו ורטרייבן׳ זינטמול גאט דער הער אונש אויף גיליגט הוט׳ אונטר איינן כוס עקסעמפל׳ ורשפרייט צו זיין׳ דא מיט אידר מעניגליכן איין משל וצעתי׳ וויא גאט דער הער׳ דיא שטרופט וועלכר זיין גיבאט כיט האלטן׳ אונ׳ זינדיגן׳ אונ׳ קיין ואלק ורשונט׳ דן ער אונש יודן זייני קינדר נענט׳ אונ׳ דאך איבר שו מאות שנה אין דיזם ביטרקייט לושט׳ ווען מן אונש דען זולט אלנט הלבין׳ ורשטושין אונ׳ ור יאגין׳ זא האנדלט מן דוך ווידר גוטש בישעליך׳ אונ׳ אליר נביאים פרופיציאונג׳ זא הוט אויך ישוע נוצרי כיט האבין וועלן דש מן אונש ורשטושין אודר ורדערבן זולי׳ דען וויא אוש אוין גיליון גשריבן הוט ער זעלבשטן ואר אונש גיבעטן אונ׳ זאגט כהאי לישנא

אך

Yudisher Theriak

This is a remedy and a beneficial book.

With it, every ordinary Jewish man and woman will be able to purge and defend against the Christians with truth, and respond with proofs from the Torah, Prophets, Mishnah, Talmud, and other decisors. They will also be able to give *proofs from Christian scholars and books.*[1]

The apostate, "Samael"[2] Friedrich Brenz from Oettingen, has falsely accused the Jews in his newly published book called *The Jewish Stripped-off Snakeskin.*[3]

Adorned with nice concordances and source references. Also, listed in the back are paragraph references for the whole book where everything can be found.

To honor all men and women, in good High German,[4] so that it will be possible to understand and be of use. There is nothing like it in print.

By Zalman Zvi of Aufhausen, under the Schenkenstein.[5] Composed and prepared for publication in seven chapters.

Here in the holy community of Hanau.

With the approval of his majesty, the noble lord. *Rosh Hodesh Adar* II, 5375 [1615].

Cum licentia Superiorum.

---

1. The book has many phrases that are in Hebrew rather than Yiddish. I have italicized these passages to highlight them.
2. His actual name was Samuel. "Samael" is a name for Satan in Talmudic literature.
3. It is usually abbreviated to *Schlangenbalg* in the text.
4. "Gut Hoch Teitsch" can mean either High German or Yiddish. This phrase is particularly interesting, as his language is neither pure Yiddish nor pure German but something in between.
5. This is Burg Schenkenstein, a castle that sits above the village of Aufhausen, which today is a suburb of the city of Bopfingen (Ostalbkreis) in Baden Württemberg, near the Bavarian border.

Proverbs of Solomon

Elijah the Tishbyite, priest and prophet, zealot, attack my enemies, every captain of fifty.[1]

Give assistance to your brother, the son of Eleazar, Solomon Zvi, a non-priest, to eat sanctified food.[2]

An apostate has arisen, from the best of their vanities; he took hold of their laws, a new one, he came but lately.[3]

He will darken the lights; will denigrate the teachings that were said at Sinai, with torches and earthquakes.[4]

He published books, wanton statements, that we curse the nobles and insult their religion.

They devastate lands, sorcerers and thieves; they kill with falsehoods, the sons of Dan, Hushim.[5]

This poem is written in Hebrew in the *Azharot* style. For details on this style of *piyyut*, see Israel Zinberg, *History of Jewish Literature* (Cincinnati: Hebrew Union College Press, 1975), 7:165. The sentence structure is sometimes rearranged to fit the poetic form. "Zalman" is the Yiddish version of "Solomon."

1. Leader of fifty soldiers; an allusion to 2 Kings 1:10. Throughout this translation, paraphrases or indirect allusions to biblical verses as well as nonbiblical sources will be cited in endnotes; exact biblical quotations will be cited in the text in brackets.
2. The allusion is to the rabbinic tradition that Elijah was the same person as Phinehas, the son of Eleazar, the son of the high priest Aaron.
3. Deuteronomy 32:17. The citations are often paraphrases or allusions to the cited verses.
4. An allusion to Exodus 19:18–19.
5. Genesis 46:23.

Without reason, the dullard brings forth slander,[6] past and future, without knowledge and guilt.

It crossed his mind to wage war with all his strength, against God and His anointed one, with contradictory falsehoods.

And I, like a wall, in form and stature, will battle against him, and I will engage the serpents.

Samael Friedrich, like a serpent in the road,[7] your fear grips them, and the way of women.[8]

If you will strike at my heel,[9] and disgrace me, you will not wear me out; I will put balm on my wounds.[10]

I will light my candle, for every Israelite man, who will taste the balm, sweet to the palates of people.

The upright will praise, for generations, He who formed the mountains,[11] like the pleasing odor of the offerings.[12]

I donned a garment of light,[13] of the masters of the Torah, and with the authority of the government, I will hasten as a shock-troop,[14]

To the creation of the earth, five thousand, and three hundred and seventy-five,[15] may He have compassion on Zion, may the abandoned be gathered.

---

6. Proverbs 10:18.
7. Genesis 49:17.
8. The phrase "the way of women" is first found in Genesis 31:35. It refers to a woman's menstrual period. There is a concept in the Christian *Adversus Judaeos* literature that Jewish men menstruate like women. This phrase may be a reference to that calumny. On this issue in the early modern period, see David S. Katz, "Shylock's Gender: Jewish Male Menstruation in Early Modern England," *Review of English Studies* 50, no. 200 (November 1999): 440–62.
9. Genesis 3:15.
10. Jeremiah 51:8.
11. Amos 4:13.
12. Exodus 29:18.
13. Psalms 104:2.
14. Numbers 32:17.
15. The Hebrew letters that have the numerical value 375 also spell out "Solomon," the author's name. This is equivalent to the year 1615 on the Christian calendar.

Introduction of the Author Solomon

I said in my wisdom, "*A time for silence and a time for speaking*" [Ecclesiastes 3:7].

There is a time to be silent. There is also a time to speak. Everything has its time. Silence is very good. Speaking is much better when it fills a need.

Ecclesiastes 3.[1]

It is not always done well when one is silent. When someone impugns your honor and respect, calls you a thief, murderer, and similar things, if you want to remain silent, you do not do well thereby. Through your silence you cause listeners to believe this about you, suspect the innocent, and sin through your silence. You also cause shame and derision for your pious parents under the earth, your children, and future descendants with your silence. Each person is especially responsible to respond, as it is written, "*You shall be clear before the Lord and before Israel*" [Numbers 32:22]. You should be free and pure before God and people. When you are certain before God in Heaven, you should also purify yourself, purging and responding to people. These and similar parables and examples aroused and awakened me, Zalman Zvi, to speak and to open all the old wrongs and abscesses, since everybody knows how much the apostates or baptized Jews, in Germany, wrote poisonous, empty, and false books against us and prepared them for publication. They accuse us of every blasphemy in them. However, nobody has ventured to write against them, perhaps to please the others. Unlike our pious ones, like Josephus, who wrote against a Greek who was called Apion, and who falsely accused us Jews. He wrote

Silence is not always good.

1. Throughout this translation, the phrases that appear in these marginal notes indicate notes and phrases that were printed in the margins of the original text. They will be inserted where they are found in the original text.

fifty pages against him. You can find them in *Josephus, the Romans*. I want to follow this one and similar honest men (I have no desire to compare myself to such worthy men). I took to heart how, in this year, an apostate by the name of Samael Friedrich Brenz from Oettingen printed a book with many pages, in thousands of copies.

The apostate from Oettingen cursed all Jews as witches, thieves, and blasphemers. He also accused Jews of the blood libel. We curse emperor and king, heaven forbid.

In it, he accuses all ordinary Jews of being witches, blasphemers, thieves, robbers, murderers, adulterers, and every other depravity. He was also not silent and accused us, contrary to the declarations and charters of the pope and emperors, may their glory be exalted, of the blood libel. He also falsely declared that we curse the emperor, king, and nobles, may their glory be exalted. It is no wonder that Christians, noble and common, are against us, and caused not a few inappropriate and angry suspicions. If ten people who understand did not believe it, the populace and simple, ordinary people who do not view the Jews favorably believed it. It was placed before me, and worthy people waved it under my nose. As a result I called the aforementioned apostate a liar, as I continue to do to the present. On Monday, the seventh of *Ab*, he[2] rode up to my door in a violent manner and threatened me and wanted to kill me. He publicly confirmed the wickedness of his book in front of Jews and Christians, said that it was all true and just, and wanted to continue persecuting Jews. However, I sanctified the name of God in response to his desecration of God's name and called him a liar to his face and swore to write a book against his lies, in a similar form, and to prepare it for publication. I wrote concerning this to almost all of the sages of Israel in the holy communities of Germany and Prague, and implored them regarding this matter. Those who responded appropriately still placed the yoke on my neck.

Zalman suffered fearsome troubles because of this book.

The Holy One, who knows everything, knows that I had to endure a great and painfully exhausting task, over long distances, spending much money and working more than three-quarters of a year. I left my wife and six small children behind, hungry and naked, in a time of misery and high prices. They and I endured much privation and anguish to put this on paper. However, I have God Almighty, who loves all people, and like Abraham our father, either sacrifice the children, or transgress His command. I cast my wife and children to the wind to make it possible for me to write this tractate and book. As much as was possible for me, I described everything that came from this lying apostate's mouth, word for word what he wrote against us, and I have written a response to it. I have also

2. A reference to S. F. Brenz.

brought proofs from the Torah, Prophets, and Writings, Mishnah, Talmud, Decisors.

I also read other books by Christian scholars, the Gospels themselves, and traveled to many places, to prove my words with truth. With this the Christians will feel and see that these accusations and evil things are, thank God, empty. I also know that I have not written everything correctly.

Zalman brings his evidence from Jewish and Christian books.

For some, it will be too brief; for others, too long. I must leave it as it is. Even Moses our teacher could not do right. "*God requires the heart.*"[3] My intentions are good. Whoever does not accept it, what can I do? Though I am not the greatest scholar, there are many in Israel, because of our many sins, who know less in Mishnah, Bible, and Talmud. However, I am more specially qualified for this work than the great scholars of the world. If, heaven forbid, I would want to do it, it is no shame for Jews.

Moses our teacher could not do the right thing for everyone; how much less so Zalman Zvi.

They can say that if Zalman Aufhausen has spoken improperly, he is no rabbi. However, if I speak properly, as I hope, then Jews can boast that such an ordinary person can produce such a work. Properly educated Jews should judge, as in the story of Gebiha, son of Pesisa, in the chapter "*All of Israel have a share.*"[4] However, through my suffering and misfortune, because of our many sins, I had to move to foreign lands for many years. Evil Jews chased me away after they took away what was mine. They saw my tears and misfortune and laughed. I am also more experienced than others in the languages and writing of the Christians. I have dared to honor with this book, in Hebrew/Yiddish and Latin alphabets, men and women, Jews and Christians. I have composed it and had it published in seven chapters. Not all things are in the vernacular but were written in High German [Hoch Teutsch]. Therefore one should not as is customary rumble about it, but read it diligently. I have added all the source citations, where each verse or citation can be found, and placed concordances in the margins, which show the contents there. With this, one can quickly and easily find what one needs. I offered it and did not want to spare either money or paper, in the hope that every Jew who can read Yiddish and pious Christians who like to pick up Latin alphabet books [can read

It is better that Zalman wrote this book than greater Torah scholars.

3. B. *Sanhedrin* 106b.
4. B. *Sanhedrin* 91a. In the Talmudic story, Gebiha is an ordinary Jew who defends the doctrine of the resurrection of the dead against a heretic who denigrated the doctrine.

it]; [it is] not a small thing, and [it is offered] for the sake of truehearted men who went before me. With this, through a part of my exertion, this blessed work was completed. I have not scorned the great ones, may God protect them, in this work. I have not written this, much less, for my glory or haughtiness, as God knows.

This book is a necessity and a defense.

[This book is intended] only as a definitive purgative and beneficial remedy against the poisonous book *The Jewish Stripped-off Snakeskin*, as the apostate called his book. Therefore I named my book the *Jewish Remedy*, which is a healing balm and beneficial medicine for this existing poison. You will accept it lovingly and remember me for good. Since it is impossible, as Ecclesiastes writes, that a man full of vexation can write so beautifully clear and thoughtfully, like someone who lives in peace, as we find in our Prophets, "*As the musician played, the hand of the Lord came upon him*" [2 Kings 3:15]. I have taken this as my summary. The pious will apply this to me. Evil people will speak against me. God will bend the hearts of all Jews and Christians to live according to His divine will, and wish all much peace, amen. *So desires for every reader, your servant*, Zalman Zvi Aufhausen.

CHAPTER 1

Herein we Jews demonstrate that the apostate from Oettingen, Samael Friedrich Brenz, accuses us falsely and says, heaven forbid, that we are blasphemers, sorcerers, and other terrible things that he lied about us. We will respond to these lies with Truth and with clear proofs from the Torah, Prophets, Writings, and also from the Talmud. The apostate's lies will be thrust back into his bosom, and will in addition show that he is an ignoramus and a thick boor.

First principle. Why we bring proofs from the Talmud.

Know that the apostate in his book of lies, the *Schlangenbalg*, reports in chapter 6, paragraph 3, that we rely more on the Talmud than on the Torah of Moses our teacher, of blessed memory. If so he admits that we Jews consider everything that is written in it to be true, and each Jew is obligated to follow it. As he writes in that chapter and paragraph, it is a law from Moses on Sinai; whoever does not observe the words of the sages, he is a heretic. Therefore we bring proofs from the Talmud. For example, he writes, the Jews do this or that. Their books and rabbis allow doing everything evil to Christians. Therefore I come here with the Talmud and prove the opposite, and *keep this principle in hand. This is sufficient for the wise.*

Second principle.

Where I write in this book *Schlangenbalg*, I mean the poisonous book that the apostate wrote. I call him "Samael"; *he is as his name, and he is the apostate.* From time to time, I call him a liar, or *the primordial serpent.*[1] Wherever you find this language, understand that I mean the apostate.

Third principle.

The apostate divided his book, *Schlangenbalg*, into seven chapters, and wrote his evil things. So I have also divided my book into seven chapters.

1. This is an allusion to the serpent in the Garden of Eden.

Where he begins a chapter, I have also begun mine. Where he ends, I also end mine. I bring all of his evil, word for word, as he expressed it. I respond to everything, small and large.

The apostate wrote his evil book without any order.

However, the apostate ignoramus wrote his book without any order, and mixed all of his messages together. Now he writes about faith, and afterward he writes about witchcraft. Now he writes about stealing, and afterward about murder. Now again about faith, and then about curses. The end of the matter is that he jumbles it all together. So I must also follow his order and must have great exertion and work.

Zalman needed much work for this book.

If he had assembled his topics, like witchcraft, murder, stealing, curses, and things similar to them, each one separately, I would have been able to explain five lies with one explanation. Therefore I have divided my chapters and identified each matter with paragraph numbers, 1, 2, 3. Thus when the apostate cites a matter that he previously discussed, and has been responded to, then I write that in this chapter, in this paragraph, it was answered. So you can find it with little work and exertion. Therefore I have also noted the sources of all verses and texts, so that it can easily be noted.

IN THE NAME OF THE LORD WHO EXAMINES HEARTS,
I WILL CONTRADICT THE ONE WHO SPEAKS FALSEHOOD,
FROM THE WORTHLESS I WILL PRODUCE WHAT IS NOBLE[2]

1

That we should not denigrate Christians and their messiah.

Know that our sages, of blessed memory, according to no book allowed or ordered us to disdain or to mock, much less curse, those who believe in Yeshua the Nazarene, or to insult them with word or deed. Since a long time ago, the Lord God exiled us from our holy land because of our many sins, and the Temple was destroyed. We were dispersed and distributed among all the nations, as Moses our teacher and all the prophets had foretold.

At present, the Christians have the authority from God, and they justly rule over us, as our sages write, that we behave with respect to the kingdom. We should show honor and obedience to the emperor, dukes, and all nobles, as will be described extensively in its proper place. How can we

2. These three lines are paraphrases of Jeremiah 17:10, 9:4, and 15:19, respectively.

despise the authority of the Christians or their faith? The one who does this, he despises God, the Lord who gives out the authority.

Christians should also not do evil to the Jews, since they act against their messiah. Yeshua the Nazarene does not want that one should do evil to Jews. He says that they erred without evil intent in his death.

Christians cannot defend or find in their religion reasons to harm or expel us Jews. Since long ago, the Lord God has imposed on us that we be dispersed among you as an example, that everyone should take as an example how the Lord God punishes those who do not keep His laws and sin. No nation is exempt. He called us Jews His children, and yet has kept us in servitude for fifteen hundred years. When we are kept in misery, expelled and chased out, one acts against God's commands, and all prophets prophesy this. Yeshua the Nazarene also did not want that we should be expelled or destroyed. It is written in the Gospels, he himself commanded us, and said in the following language, "*O Father, forgive them, since they do not know what they are bringing upon me.*"[3] Christians recognize that it is clear that all of this had to happen. With this, the law was fulfilled, and they would be saved. Therefore both Testaments tell us that we should not be enemies. Both sides should place these things before the true judge and not engage in evil activities against each other. This should all be extensively written about, as it will come to pass.

We call Yeshua the Nazarene *Tola*.

The apostate from Oettingen writes in the beginning of his chapter that we call Christ the *Tola*. This means someone hanged, like any other evildoer. Concerning this I say, a man in the world who understands the Holy Tongue should come and translate the word *Tola*. The ignoramus writes *Tola* with an *ayin* at the end. This is a worm or the color scarlet.

Lamentations 4.

In Lamentations 4 it is written, "*Those who were reared in scarlet*" [Lamentations 4:5]. This is, those who were reared in scarlet cling to ash heaps.

Genesis 24.[4]

"*Tola, Puvah, Iob, and Shimron*" [Genesis 46:13]. These were the sons of Issachar.

Judges 10.

Tola, the son of Puah, was a judge in Israel.[5] If *Tola* had meant "hanged man," would Issachar have named his son "one who was hanged"? Similarly, the judge in Israel. I write this only so that the apostate's stupidity can be recognized.

3. A paraphrase of Luke 23:34. Translations from the New Testament are from the NRSV.
4. This is a mistake. It should be Genesis 46.
5. Judges 10:1.

The fool had meant and wanted to say that we call Yeshua the Nazarene "hanged" [*Taluy*]. This indeed means "one who was hanged." However, not "one worthy of being hanged." It is not a negative, mocking, or shameful reference to him.

Taluy. The word does not mean that someone was hanged because of evil deeds.[6]

The Christians themselves say that he was crucified. No evil or dishonor can be taken or understood from the word *Taluy*. Many of our high nobles were hanged. It is written in 2 Samuel 21 how seven innocent children of King Saul and friends were hanged because of the Gibeonites, and all were innocent. We also call them *hanged*, or *impaled*. They are the hanged ones, as the verse says, "*They gathered the bones of those who had been impaled*" [2 Samuel 21:13]. They gathered the bones of those who had been hanged.

2 Samuel 21, there.

If it were as the apostate, the distorter of truth, writes, the verse would have had to say, "the bones of the evildoers worthy of being hanged." Heaven forbid, they were pious and innocent royal children, and they were properly buried. Thus it can never be demonstrated that the term *Taluy* can have the meaning of "worthy of being hanged" or "evildoer" in referring to him. Ordinary Jews also call the Christian messiah "Yeshua the Nazarene." However, ordinary people use a shorthand term, *Taluy*. This expression is meant everywhere as a term of uncertainty, since the Christians consider him to be a god.

Taluy is translated as "uncertain"; chapter "Which was the place."[6]

The Turks and other nations argue against it. Since there is a difference of opinion and uncertainty, so we call Christ *Taluy*.

This uncertainty is expressed in Hosea 11. "*For My people persists in its defection from Me*" [Hosea 11:7]. This means, My people are uncertain about returning to Me. *Our eyes are raised up to you*. Our eyes hope for you. These words cannot be translated as "being guilty of hanging."[7]

Hosea 11.

6. B. *Zevahim*, chapter 5. Before the standardization of Talmudic pages in the Daniel Bomberg edition, Talmudic citations were made according to chapter name. Zalman Zvi uses both systems of citation, sometimes one and sometimes the other. The older system of citation continued to be used well into the seventeenth century.

7. Both the biblical verse and the liturgical phrase that he also quotes in Hebrew use a version of the word *Taluy*. His purpose is to show that it is used in Jewish contexts without negative associations.

2

Our sages also use the term *Taluy* for uncertainty. They say, "*A sin offering for a nazirite, a sin offering for leprosy, a sin offering for uncertain guilt.*" *A sin offering for uncertain guilt* does not mean the offering for someone guilty of hanging. Rather, it is an offering for uncertainty, as when someone made a mistake. He ate forbidden fat, and he had thought that he had eaten permitted fat.[8] For this one had to bring a sacrifice that was called "*the sin offering of uncertainty.*" This is the sacrifice of uncertainty. Therefore we Jews, at a minimum, do not disdain their messiah when we call him *Taluy*. *With this, it is enough. I have gone on at length with the balm that I have prepared for the Christians.*

The apostate writes in his book, *Schlangenbalg*, that we call Christ "Jesus the Nazarene." This is spiteful, and we leave out the best letter, that is the *ayin*.[9] I say that all the scholars of the Hebrew language should show if this is a contemptible thing. Jesus the Nazarene is the name that Christians themselves give him. Nazareth is the name of the city where his parents were born. However, in the Hebrew language, *Nozri* [Nazarene] can be translated as "guard" or "watchman," as [the verse says], "*the day . . . when watchmen shall proclaim . . . come, let us go up*" [Jeremiah 31:6]. This means, the day that the watchmen will call, come, let us go up, etc.

Below, in chapter 5, paragraph 4; the apostate says that we call him "Yeshua," with an ayin.

"*Extending kindness to the thousandth generation*" [Exodus 34:7]. That is, he keeps it to a thousand generations. The word *nozer* [extends] is a consolation and a good, noble word for us people. It is not despicable, as the apostate writes. No person on the earth would explain Jesus of Nazareth in any other way. Someone born in Jerusalem is called a Jerusalemite. Who can protect themselves against a false, invalid tongue?

3

The apostate writes that we call Yeshua the Nazarene a "bastard son of a menstruant." That is, the son of a whore who was conceived and born in

8. For example, *Genesis Rabbah* 44.14.

9. The issue is theological rather than linguistic. *Yeshu*, which I have translated as "Jesus," is a hebraization of the Greek name *Jesu*. Jesus' Hebrew name should be *Yeshua*, or Joshua, which in Hebrew means "salvation." Without the *ayin*, which is the last letter of *Yeshua*, the name becomes *Yeshu*. Brenz is trying to argue that Jews deny Jesus as savior, and that is why they use the name *Yeshu* rather than *Yeshua*.

impurity. I say that I will show all the following from the apostate's own words that he is lying, since he writes the following, with these words.

In paragraph 5. The Jews say that if the hanged one had done good, there would not have been any Jew who would not have given him his daughter as a wife. See that, if we consider him a bastard, how then could an important Jew have given him his daughter as a wife? Even the most lax one would not have intermarried with him.

Deuteronomy 23. There is in the Torah of Moses, in Deuteronomy 23, "*No bastard can come into the congregation of the Lord*" [23:2]. That is, a child of a whore should not come into the community of God, also to the tenth generation. On the other hand, our sages, of blessed memory, write nothing about this in the Talmud. They also write that we should also not despise him.

Genesis 9. Our sages write this explanation concerning the verse,[10] "*But for your own life-blood I will require a reckoning, etc.*" [Genesis 9:5]. This is, "I will examine your own blood from your soul." This is, when somebody willingly puts himself in danger, and through this he loses his life. So God, blessed be He, demands from one who has such a death that he will be condemned and destroyed in the next world. How should we be against God's command about life and limb and all welfare, and so wantonly and lightly hang the Christian messiah on nails with such public disdain?

Psalms 34. Does it not also say, "*Guard your tongue from evil, etc.*" [Psalms 34:14]. Guard your tongue from speaking evil, etc. How should we speak about a thing that is such a great danger, and does not help us? Further on, the apostate wants to say that we do this among ourselves secretly. So I say that this cannot be, since we know that daily there are those among us who allow themselves to be baptized. They tell the worst lies about us. It will be discussed at greater length in the places where it will occur.

4

The apostate writes further in his *Schlangenbalg*. When a Jew wants to disparage and deride another Jew, he says to him, "O you Jesus the Nazarene." About this I say I have rarely heard this. It might sometimes happen that someone speaks in this way, however, not to disparage or to mock.

10. B. *Sanhedrin* 57b is the closest likely source.

Rather, in this way. When someone sees on the Sabbath that someone comes home late on Friday, or he talks excessively about business on the Sabbath, or he publicly says, "I will do this tomorrow," which we all consider the desecration of the Sabbath and a great sin, which because of our sins happens often, if a pious person sees this, he might well say, "O you Jesus the Nazarene." You are like Jesus the Nazarene, in that you do not keep the Sabbath. Rather, you think that everything is permitted to be done on the Sabbath.

You can light a fire and work if you want to, as is found in Gospels Matthew,[11] Luke,[12] and Mark,[13] that Yeshua of Nazareth and his disciples were going through a wheat field on the Sabbath. His disciples tore off some stalks and ate them. The Pharisees (that is to say, the *Perushim*) spoke against it. Jesus of Nazareth said: "I am the Lord of the Sabbath." In this manner, he might say, "O, you are Jesus the Nazarene, the Lord of the Sabbath?" However, this is not to be disparaging or mocking. However, when men or women who do not understand use such words, they do it without understanding, and no honest Jew likes this. Further, saying this, one is not faithful to our books.

Matthew 12; Luke 6; Mark 2.

It also sometimes occurs when someone comes and wants to make everyone healthy or to distribute a remedy and salve for all illnesses. Someone might say, "He is Jesus the Nazarene"; this means Jesus from Nazareth. He wants to heal all illnesses with one means and one remedy.

5

Secondly, *Schlangenbalg* writes: When one among us is found who does not want to do good, we say, "He does good like the hanged one." We say along with it when this hanged one did good. There was no Jew in Israel who wanted to give him his daughter as a wife. Here, he calls himself a liar.

Above, in paragraph 3, the apostate says that we consider him and call him a bastard, son of a menstruant. If so, how should we have given him a daughter? Indeed, he wanted to do evil, as has been written at length above, since it was not commanded to us to despise him.

Above, paragraph 3.

11. Matthew 12:1–5.
12. Luke 6:1–5.
13. Mark 2:23–28.

6

The apostate writes further in his *Schlangenbalg*, a long piece of nonsense and foolishness, and says that we say that God sent Yeshua the Nazarene to Rome and ordered that he should publicly confess that he was not the Messiah. If so, he would no longer be judged or tormented. Rather, he would be free of his suffering. I have never heard of this nonsense nor seen it written in any book. The apostate should write or show where it is written.

The apostate says further. When one Jew sees another one waking up early, he says to the other one that he has seen: "See, you woke up before the hanged one paid a visit." We say this to mock and deride Jesus the Nazarene. Woe to the poor, blind, and foolish apostate. The Christians say this more than the Jews. Does the rogue want to compare the *tul*, that is a bird that sits on nuts, to the hanged one [*taluy*]? This bird's nature is to stretch its wings and fly back and forth before daybreak. So one sees the other one waking up early and swarming back and forth, he says to the other one, "You are awake before the '*tul.*'" That is before the bird has visited or flown around. I have heard this often where many of these birds are found. The apostate is a donkey. He can again translate according to other languages. One can find many similar fools. However, the truth is, so everyone who understands knows that I am correct.

7

The apostate cites a book, which is supposedly called *Ma'aseh Tola.*

The apostate further writes excessively long nonsense and foolishness from a book that is supposedly called *Ma'aseh Tola.*[14] He says that it was not printed but is clearly written, and we lend this in great secrecy. It is written in this book, in great detail, that Christ, who was the son of a whore, was a very good student. Once, he threw a ball on the roof, and because of this, his teacher became angry with him and said: "Stop throwing, you *bastard, son of the menstruant.*" This is, the son of a whore who was born in impurity. Because of this Jesus pestered his mother until she confessed that he was the child of a whore and that she was a whore. I say about this that in all my life I have never seen such a book. I wonder, if this book was a secret, where did the apostate see it? Is it because he had been a Jew and had been a rope-maker and a water carrier? So he could not read a word in it, much less understand it. We do not find in our Talmud or holy books one word about this foolish nonsense. If someone

14. A reference to the work better known as *Toledot Yeshu.*

would be a *bastard, son of the menstruant* because they threw a ball on the roof, then there would be very few pious children on the earth, especially in Italy and France, where they play much with balls. If I had found such a book, I would have remembered. An apostate or rogue, like Samael Friedrich, wrote about it to beat us and slander us with it. However, I studied and went through most of the Talmud with great effort and diligence, and have found ten reliable witnesses that the Jesus who is mentioned in several places in our Talmud cannot be the Jesus whom the Christians believe in. It must have been someone else who was called Jesus and was killed by Jews. I want to do this with great diligence. If you can show me the opposite, I will gladly have been mistaken.

First, all nations acknowledge and all chronicles show that the Second 1
Temple stood for 420 years and several months. Until Titus and Vespasian, the Romans, destroyed it. So writes *Seder Olam*.[15] Furthermore, the Talmud and all books [write] that Rabbi Joshua, son of Perahia, was the teacher of Yeshua of Nazareth. This rabbi, Joshua, son of Perahia, and Simeon, son of Shetah, lived in the year 3621 after creation, according to the calendar of the Jews, and 233 years after the Temple was built. This was the teacher of the Jesus who is written about in the Talmud.

This must have been another Jesus. The Second Temple, four hundred and twenty years. Joshua, son of Perahiah, the teacher of Jesus, lived 3,621 years after creation, 233 years after the building of the Second Temple. Yeshua the Nazarene was born in the times of King Herod and Hillel and Shammai, 130 years after the first Jesus.

However, the Yeshua of Nazareth whom Christians believe in and according to the Gospels was born in the time of King Herod. Hillel and Shammai lived during the same time, fully 130 years after the above-mentioned Joshua, son of Perahiah, who was the teacher of that Jesus mentioned in the Talmud.[16] I will demonstrate the generations and lineages later.

See, it is written in *Pirke Avot*, chapter 1. Simeon the Righteous was from the Great Assembly.[17] He was a member of the Great Assembly who went out of Babylon with Ezra to Jerusalem. They established our prayers. This Simeon the Righteous lived in the time of Alexander of Macedon, as Josephus writes in *Josephus, the Romans*. Josephus and Alexander of Macedon called this Simeon "Judeo," and held him in high regard, as all the chronicles write. This was one generation or period.

***Pirke Avot*, chapter 1.**

Simeon the Righteous. Ezra and his court established our prayers.

15. *Seder Olam* is a midrashic chronological work that is the basis for much of rabbinic historiography.

16. The story of Jesus' being his disciple is found in B. *Sotah* 47a.

17. M. *Avot* 1.2. The information he provides about these figures is not found in M. *Avot* but rather drawn from other sources.

Second generation, Antigonus of Socho.

The second generation or period was Antigonus of Socho.[18] In his times the cursed *Zedukim* began. The nations and the Christians in the Gospels call them "Sadducees."

The third generation, Yohanan, son of Yoezer,[19] and Yohanan of Jerusalem.

The third generation or period was Yose, son of Yoezer of Zeredah, and Yohanan of Jerusalem.[20]

The fourth generation, Joshua, son of Perahiah, the teacher of Jesus, 207 years before the destruction of the Second Temple.

After them was Joshua, son of Perahiah.[21] He was the teacher of Jesus, about whom the Talmud writes that he was an antinomian.[22] This was 207 years before the destruction of the Second Temple.

The fifth generation, Judah, son of Tabbai, and Simeon, son of Shetah.[23]

The sixth generation, Shemaiah and Abtalion.

The sixth generation was Shemaiah and Abtalion.[24]

The seventh generation was Hillel and Shammai. They lived at the end of King Herod's reign. During that time, Yeshua of Nazareth was born in Bethlehem in Judea. With this, Jews and Christians are in agreement.

Two generations between one Jesus, who was the disciple of Rabbi Joshua, son of Perahiah, until Yeshua of Nazareth and more than 130 years.

Thus we find that there are two generations between the Joshua of Perahiah who was the teacher of Jesus until Hillel and Shammai, in the time of Herod. Only in this period was the Christian Yeshua born and was put to death in Jerusalem under Pontius Pilate. The calculation is more than 130 years from Rabbi Joshua, son of Perahiah, the teacher of Jesus, until the birth of Jesus, the Christian messiah. So Yeshua of Nazareth must have been more than 130 years old. Everyone knows that he was thirty-three years old when he was condemned. This is a strong proof that the Jesus the Talmud writes about was another Jesus.

The second testimony, *Sanhedrin* 44.

Secondly, the Talmud says in *Sanhedrin* 44.[25] It speaks there about the instigator. There was one who was called Jesus. First he was stoned, and afterward he was hanged. Yet Yeshua of Nazareth was hanged alive according to the words of the Gospels.

---

18. M. *Avot* 1.3.
19. A mistake. It should be Yose, son of Yoezer.
20. M. *Avot* 1.4. It should be Yose, son of Yohanan of Jerusalem.
21. M. *Avot* 1.6.
22. B. *Sotah* 47a.
23. M. *Avot* 1.8.
24. M. *Avot* 1.10.
25. It should be B. *Sanhedrin* 43a.

It is written in the above-mentioned place. They called out publicly for forty days in a row that Jesus would be stoned. Whoever could find any merit or good for him and give truthful testimony that he was innocent should come and report this.

The third testimony, there.

The Yeshua that the Christians believe in was quickly and without delay captured and was put to death the next day, according to the Gospels Matthew, Mark, and Luke.

The fourth testimony. The Talmud writes in the above-mentioned place in *Sanhedrin*. Jesus had five disciples, but Jesus the Nazarene had twelve disciples.

The fourth testimony, there.

The fifth testimony there. He mentions the five disciples by name. The first was called Mati; the second Khakai; the third Nezar; the fourth Bunin; the fifth Todah.

Fifth testimony, there.

The disciples of Jesus of Nazareth did not have these names. Rather, Yohanan, Peter, Paulus, Lukas, Martin,[26] Judas, etc.

The sixth testimony. It is written in the above-mentioned Talmud that all five of the disciples were condemned in Jerusalem, because of the accusations by the Jews. However, the disciples of Jesus of Nazareth were condemned here and there by pagan kings; as can be found in the histories of the apostles.

Sixth testimony. Pagan kings condemned the disciples of Jesus the Nazarene.

The Talmud also writes there that Jesus was condemned according to the laws of the Torah. He was stoned and afterward he was hanged. However Jesus of Nazareth, who was condemned under the authority of Pontius Pilate, was a healer in Jerusalem when the Romans occupied it. Yeshua the Nazarene was judged and hanged alive on the cross, which is against the laws of the Torah and all Jewish practice. This is completely against Jewish law. We do not have more than the four modes of death when someone was condemned, as is written in the Torah. They are: *stoning*, *burning*, *beheading*, and *strangulation*. This means: stoning, burning, strangulation, and beheading with the sword. However, since at this time we were under the domination of the Romans, the Romans

Seventh testimony.

26. The Yiddish text has "Martin." One would have thought the author meant to refer to Matthew. This may be an error by the printer, who misread the name; in all other places Zalman Zvi cites Matthew.

killed him on the cross while still alive, according to their practice, which under them was very cruel. Josephus writes and tells how he was once traveling and found several of his acquaintances hanging on crosses, though they were still alive, and he freed them. So we can see that the Jesus whom the Talmud writes about could not be the Christian messiah.

Eighth testimony. Jesus was captured in Lod and judged there.

Eighth. In many editions of the Talmud, *Sanhedrin* 67, it is written that Jesus was captured and condemned in Lod, in a city of that name.[27] However, Yeshua of Nazareth was arrested and judged in Jerusalem, as Christians and Jews acknowledge.

Ninth testimony.

Ninth. It is written that the father of Jesus was called "Papus, the son of Judah."[28] Mary's fiancé was called "Joseph," as is written in the Gospels.

Tenth testimony, *Sotah* 47.

Tenth. It is written in the Talmud, *Sotah* 47. Jesus set up a brick as an idol and worshiped it.[29] We find nowhere that Jesus, the Christian messiah, worshiped any idols or called to anyone other than the Father. Thus we can see the difference between the Jesus written about in the Talmud and the Christian messiah. I find it impossible that this Jesus refers to the one in whom the Christians believe. If nothing else, the first proof shows that Joshua, son of Perahiah, and Simeon, son of Shetah, were in the time of the Hasmoneans, whom the Christians call the Maccabees. During that time were also Ezra and his community, who established our prayers. This was not long after the redemption from Babylon, in the time of Simeon the Righteous. Josephus and all trustworthy books show this. So too, the Jesus about whom the Talmud writes was also at the same time, fully 130 years before Yeshua of Nazareth, the Christian messiah, who lived in the times of Herod and Hillel and Shammai. He was born not long before the destruction of the Temple. Therefore I say again before my gentle people that our Talmud talked about a different Jesus. Thus we do not find anything about his history, only what Josephus wrote in his book for the Romans. Here he

---

27. This story is found in uncensored manuscripts of the Talmud. The Soncino translation of the Talmud, *Sanhedrin* 67a, n. 12, cites R. T. Herford, *Christianity in Talmud and Midrash* (Hoboken, NJ: Ktav Publishing, 1975), 37, as the source.
28. Ibid.
29. B. *Sotah* 47a. The disciple in this story is called "Jesus" in uncensored versions of the Talmud.

mentions something about John the Baptist, but our ancestors write nothing about Yeshua, the Christian messiah.

The reason why nothing is written in the books about Yeshua the Nazarene.

The reason is that no Jews worshiped with him. Someone might have easily written instead that this was something bad for us, as unfortunately happens to us daily. Our ancestors and Talmudists saw that the Christian religion grew stronger from day to day. So they refrained as much as they could from this argument.

8

The apostate writes about why the priests are called priests.

Schlangenbalg writes further in his book. We called the Catholic priests *galohim*. This means "shaved ones." He shows that we supposedly say: Yeshua the Nazarene ran into the Temple and stole the Ineffable Name. He cut open his calf, and sewed it inside. After he ran out, he ripped the calf open, took out the Name, and performed many wonders with the Name, and he flew in the air. Afterward, our rabbis wrote the Ineffable Name on a Jew's back, and caused him to fly over him. He urinated on him.[30] Therefore Yeshua the Nazarene fell and crashed to the ground. He fell into a corner. His adherents and disciples hurried over and grabbed him by the hair and wanted to pull him out. They tore his hair out, and he got a bald spot. Therefore, to this day, the priests have a bald spot. The apostate says all of this, and I say I have never heard this nonsense, much less seen it written. We are not so childish to believe such foolishness. One couldn't dream of anything more foolish.

Why the priests were shaven.

Why then do the priests shave? I believe it is because they have learned from our Levites, from Numbers 8. "*Let them go over their whole body with a razor*" [Numbers 8:7]. The Levites were also shaven.

The apostate ignoramus writes further about the Ineffable Name and Kabbalah. Though he cannot read four words in a punctuated prayerbook, he writes that it would be too long for him to write about it, so he does not want to write it. *Apostate, what do you have to do with Holy things? Confine yourself to Negaim.*[31]

30. The purpose of this was to cause him to become ritually impure and render the Ineffable Name unusable.
31. A paraphrase of a rebuke in B. *Sanhedrin* 38b meaning, "Don't talk about things you know nothing about."

The apostate writes about why the people of Worms are not allowed to sweep their synagogue.

Now the *Schlangenbalg* writes a nice piece of foolishness. He says he decided of his own free will and went to Worms to visit the synagogue, since we consider it like a small temple.[32] The Jews do not sweep out any spiderwebs, since they say that God, blessed be He, rests there in a spiderweb. Once somebody wanted to sweep them out, and the vault began to move and seemed about to fall. *In the book that I prepared for the Christians*, I mocked the apostate greatly for his long journey and foolishness, and let him know that the Holy One does not rest in a spiderweb or a poisonous *Schlangenbalg*. "*Even the heavens to their uttermost reaches cannot contain You*" [1 Kings 8:27]. *He dwells in heaven and* "*His Temple is in Zion*" [Psalms 76:3].

However, why the people of Worms do not sweep, they know better than I do. It is not against [the principle of] lowering something in holiness after raising it.[33] It is not one of the Thirteen Principles that a Jew needs to know.[34]

10

The apostate writes now that we Jews wake up on the day after Yom Kippur in the name of Satan. Then we publicly confess that Satan is our father, heaven forbid. I say that we wake up in the name of the God of Israel and not in the name of Satan. However, we must fear these days more than others because the Satan stands behind us and searches all of our sins and brings them before God, as with Job, since the day of final sealing has not yet passed. Therefore we must be careful, *because the attribute of judgment is judged harshly against us in these days*. Even when a sick person first gets up from his bed, he must watch himself much more than a healthy person with unhealthy food and other things that are contrary to his complexion and nature. Otherwise he might at one time destroy what the physician had spent a long time healing in him. Satan and Samael have the habit of hindering and do not rest until they bring a

---

32. The Rashi synagogue in Worms was built in 1034 and is the oldest still-standing synagogue in Europe. *Mikdash me'at* (small temple) is a general term applied to a synagogue.
33. There is a rabbinic principle that an object can be raised to a higher level of sanctity by dedicating it to a holy purpose, but one cannot afterward use it for a less holy or secular purpose.
34. A reference to Maimonides' Thirteen Principles of Faith.

person to temptation. Therefore, we throw *the goat that is sent out*,[35] into his throat. There are also other commandments that we fulfill in order that *Satan should not prosecute us*, like blowing the ram's horn. *We all say*,

"*The Lord rebuke you, O Accuser*" [Zechariah 3:2], Samael Friedrich, apostate from Oettingen.

Deuteronomy 3.[36]

11

The apostate writes further that in previous times we made the [séance] table rise by whispering names of demons into the ears [of the demons],[37] and the table rose into the air, even when loaded with a hundredweight.

The apostate writes that the Jews make the table rise through magic.

I have written about this at length in the book that I am preparing for the Christians. I will show, not only with our books, that the Kabbalah, through holy names, is for good and not the action of demons.

Their sages and philosophers, Agrippino,[38] Theofrasto,[39] also Don Pico de-Mirandola,[40] also Doctor Reuchlin,[41] and many others also write this. It is too long to present here. All of them have experience with Kabbalah, that Kabbalah is not chiromancy or black magic. Rather it all comes from God's full authority and has no connection to the devil. Thus there can be no demonic activity with this table rising, since we sing important songs, including *Adon Olam* and *Yigdal*. No devil's work can tolerate it when God is mentioned. They only expect that everything will be evil.

Agrippino, Theofrasto, Don Pico de-Mirandola, and Doctor Reuchlin write that Kabbalah is a divine thing and not magic.

Furthermore, all kinds of magic, small and large, are forbidden on penalty of death. "*You shall not allow a sorceress to live*" [Exodus 22:17]. "*You*

Exodus 22.

35. Leviticus 16:21–22.
36. This should be Zechariah 3.
37. Knowing the name of a demon and whispering it in the demon's ear is a technique for achieving mastery over the demon and forcing it to obey one's commands.
38. Most likely Heinrich Cornelius Agrippa von Nettesheim.
39. Most likely Paracelsus, whose original name was Philippus Aureolus Theophrastus Bombastus von Hohenheim.
40. The famous Christian kabbalist Pico della Mirandola.
41. The famous Christian Hebraist Johann Reuchlin.

shall not practice divination or soothsaying, etc." [Leviticus 19:26]. "*Do not turn to ghosts and do not inquire of familiar spirits, to be defiled by them*" [Leviticus 19:31]. "*And if any person turns to ghosts and familiar spirits and goes astray after them, I will set, etc.*" [Leviticus 20:6]. "*A man or a woman who has a ghost or a familiar spirit shall be put to death, etc.*" [Leviticus 20:27].

Deuteronomy 18.

"*Let no one be found among you who consigns his son or daughter to the fire, or who is an augurer, a soothsayer, a diviner, a sorcerer*" [Deuteronomy 18:10].

Sorcery is forbidden even when no harm is caused to the person.

In conclusion, we have examples from the Torah and prophets that we should not engage in any kind of sorcery, even when it causes a loss for the person, since engaging in sorcery is forbidden to him.

It is permitted to utilize holy names.

However, it is permitted to do good with holy names and the Kabbalah, since through this one sees the powers of God. This is practical Kabbalah [*Kabbalah ma'asit*]. So when it happens that the table rises, no sorcery is needed for that. Whoever engages in sorcery is deserving of the death penalty.

***Sanhedrin* 67.**

The difference between sorcery and Kabbalah can be found in [tractate] *Sanhedrin* 67b.

12

Apostate writes that we bring the Queen of Sheba.

The apostate writes further. We bring the Queen of Sheba along with many women.[42] We dance and make merry with them. When we are finished with them, we send them back. I say about this: I do not know this, and have never seen it. However, should this be the Queen of Sheba who is written about in the Book of Kings, who gave King Solomon many gifts and brought spices?[43] If I could raise her, I do not know what I would do. First, I consider it to be sorcery; it would be against God. The world understands that bringing the Queen of Sheba is no wonder. There are people among us who do things that are against the Torah. This is very base and therefore is not of interest.

---

42. "Bring" is used in the sense of raising spirits by means of necromancy, or making the Queen of Sheba and other women appear through other forms of sorcery.

43. 1 Kings 10:1–13.

13

The apostate writes further in his book, the *Schlangenbalg*. It is found among the Jews that some take a lump of earth and make it into the form of a person. Afterward they whisper adjurations or incantations over it, and it soon lives and walks. *In the book that I have prepared for the Christians, I mocked the apostate*, and said that he himself was squeezed together and formed from street sweepings and clay, so that he can walk but has no common sense. His father might have been such a *Baal Shem*.[44] He writes that we call the concocted image *Hamor Golem*. In the language of Ashkenaz [Yiddish], this is a donkey carved out of wood.[45] *I say this is what he is*. I have not seen such a thing.

The Apostate writes that we make a *Hamor Golem*.

However, in the days of the Talmudic sages, we found such people who, with the Kabbalah and by means of the *Sefer Yezirah* [Book of Creation], created such a thing. This book was written by Abraham our patriarch, of blessed memory.[46] A part of this book is still found among us Jews. It is shown there in [tractate] *Sanhedrin* that these were through holy names and not through the actions of demons. These kabbalists secluded themselves and were compared to the prophets.

Sanhedrin 67.

So too Josephus writes in his book of the Romans about the Pharisees, Sadducees, and Essenes, that the Essenes, through their seclusion, fasting, and holiness, were able to foretell the future. However, such Kabbalah is concealed from us German Jews. However, there still may be such people in the Land of Israel who can do much with this Kabbalah. However, in these lands, we do not make our golems from clay; rather they are born from the womb.

Josephus writes about the Essenes that they prophesied.

14

The apostate writes further. The Jews place an apple in the hand of a dead person, and write devils' names on it. When the apple rots, the person

The Apostate writes that Jews kill people using the dead.

44. *Baal Shem*, literally, "master of the Name," refers to a healer who writes amulets; he uses the amulets and incantations utilizing the holy names of God and angels for healing. A *Baal Shem* would also know the holy names needed to create a golem.
45. The term *hamor* means "donkey," while the term *homer* means "clay" or "earth" in Hebrew and in Yiddish. The spelling of the two words is very similar. The emphasis is to show Brenz's ignorance of Hebrew.
46. B. *Sanhedrin* 65b.

whom they spoke evil of withers and dies. *I have written at length in the book that I have prepared for the Christians.* I curse the apostate Samael Friedrich, a knavish and malicious thief, as long as he continues to do this against the Jews. Anyone who does this, whether Christian or Jew, is a sorcerer and is deserving of the death penalty. We should not engage in any sorcery, and we also do not kill anyone through sorcery. If someone is silent about another person, he is also guilty. Sorcery applied to oneself is also forbidden, as mentioned above and will be discussed below, when we discuss "*You shall not murder*" [Exodus 21:13]. King Saul could have had all the sorcerers and necromancers, but he had them killed.

Sorcerers and necromancers are not allowed to live.

This sorcery did not hurt anyone. They only woke the dead and learned future things from them. King Saul did this and woke Samuel the prophet. He told him how Saul and his children would fall into the hands of the Philistines.

1 Samuel 21. Saul had Samuel brought up at En Dor.

God, blessed be He, did not want to answer him through the *Urim and Tumim*, as we find in 1 Samuel 21.[47] This woman was the only one left alive of the few who were familiar with this sorcery, since all the others had been killed, as we find written there. This sorcery did not harm any people. How should we kill the people of this type, heaven forbid? Therefore, God protect us.

15

The Apostate writes that the Jews kill women who have given birth and their children with sorcery.

The apostate, this infamous fellow, writes further in his book, and book of lies, the *Schlangenbalg*. When a Jewish man or woman comes into a Christian house, and a woman who has given birth is there, they take a valise lock, write names of devils on it, lock it, and throw it into a well. From this, the woman who has given birth and the child grow thin, but she must still suckle, so they must pay with their skin.[48]

Concerning this I say that a person who does such a thing is a sorcerer and should be burned. Thank God, we Jews are accused of these malevolent depravities less than any other nation or people. Balaam, an arch sorcerer who was our greatest enemy, who had wanted to curse us, gives good testimony.

---

47. The story actually occurs in 1 Samuel 28:5–25.
48. I.e., suffer the consequences.

He says in Numbers 23, "*There is no augury in Jacob*" [Numbers 23:23]. There is no sorcery in Jacob and no divining in Israel. This murderous deed is, thank God, not heard, though we go into Christian houses daily where there are women who have given birth. Our women are also brought to them for childbirths. We are in their houses, and God be praised, nothing happens to them. I say that the lying apostate Samael Friedrich Brenz is a sorcerer himself, a villainous thief, scoundrel, and murderer, as long as he says this about us Jews.

Balaam testifies that Jews are not sorcerers. Numbers 23.

One should also be careful of him that he has engaged in these things, because he writes publicly about such sorcery. He might say that he did this while he was a Jew, but he has now become pious. This is not to be believed, that murder and sorcery can be washed away by baptism. I place it before God and the courts whether the apostate should be asked further, Where had he done such things? Who were his accomplices or teachers? Anyone who does such things should be burned.

16

The *Schlangenbalg* writes further. When one of our women has a difficult delivery, we secretly write a note and put it into her mouth and her hand. From this she delivers, and he adds that this was written with Christian blood. Let all the midwives in Germany, Italy, Bohemia, Poland, Russia, and other countries give testimony here, since ordinary Christian women are midwives for our women. It happens once in a thousand times that there is a difficult delivery. We go to her with the Torah scroll, and we recite various prayers that were established for this purpose. We give charity for her sake.

The Apostate writes that the Jews need Christian blood, heaven forbid.

We write Psalm 19, "*May the Lord answer you in time of trouble*" [Psalms 20:2],[49] and other such verses from the Torah. We Jews also give this to Christians when they request it from us when their women are also in need. *I have written about this at length in the book that I have prepared for the Christians.* In Rome, Venice, Prague, Mantua, Frankfurt, Worms, and other places where there are many thousands of Jews, they use Christian midwives. Not one of them has seen such sorcery; thank God, it has never been heard of. In many places Jews have been baptized and have never

Psalm 19.

49. It was common in this period for authors to quote biblical passages from memory, and that is most likely the reason for the discrepancy.

said anything like this, much less written about it. Therefore, I pierce the heart of the scoundrel, the apostate, with the previous points.

We Jews appeal to the pope's and the emperor's declarations and confirmations about the blood.

We Jews appeal to what the pope and the emperor, his majesty, declared and confirmed, that the accusations against us Jews are, thank God, meaningless, and we are unsullied. We are also graciously protected by the emperor, dukes, and nobles from these highly punishable accusations. May they, with God's help, be brought against the apostate and not remain unanswered. I have written about this at length in the book that I have prepared for the Christians. I have described and edited the confirmations of the emperor, his majesty, concerning this matter, in this book.

17

The apostate writes that the Jews do not consider it a sin when they kill or cheat Christians.

The *Schlangenbalg* writes further. He says that we do not consider it a sin when we do anything to a Christian. So I say that many rogues are found among us who spare neither Jews nor Christians, and deceive them when they can. If I would write about where and how many times the apostate has deceived Jews and Christians, I would have to write a separate book about this. *I have written about this at length in the book that I have prepared for the Christians.* If one could assemble all the horses that the apostate had borrowed from others, one could put a regiment of riders into the field. According to my opinion, this made the apostate a Christian, since we Jews came to hate him because of this, and pushed him away with both hands, and the Christians chased him harshly.

The apostate takes interest from Christians. It will be demonstrated in chapter 3, paragraph 11.

The apostate could not leave behind the taking of interest, as will be shown in the proper time.

However, so much happens to us Jews, but the Written and Oral Torah forbid us from deceiving any person. All of the decisors also forbid this, as I will establish here with the foremost decisors.

SeMaG,[50] part 2.

SeMaG, Negative Commandments no. 2. You will find there how great a sin it is for a Jew to deceive a gentile.

There, no. 152.

You will find a long discussion of this there, in no. 152.

---

50. *SeMaG* is an abbreviation for *Sefer Mitzvot Gadol* (*The Great Book of Commandments*) by Rabbi Moses of Coucy (thirteenth century). It is an important compendium describing and analyzing the commandments.

More in *Hoshen Misphat*. Maimuni writes at the beginning of the *Laws of Theft* that it is strongly forbidden to deceive a Christian or someone of another people. *I have written about this at length and cited more sources in the book that I have prepared for the Christians* that all the decisors forbid deceiving gentiles. "*Everyone who deals dishonestly is abhorrent to the Lord your God*" [Deuteronomy 25:16]. It is abhorrent to God to deal dishonestly. These verses are familiar to Christians, since the Talmud is marked and registered, and is studied in some universities.

Hoshen Mishpat*, section 359, *Maimuni*, beginning of *Laws of Theft*.[51]

Take the Ten Statements [Ten Commandments]; also the verse, "*You shall not steal; you shall not deal deceitfully or falsely, etc.*" [Leviticus 19:11]. There is no difference between Jews and Christians; to deal unjustly is forbidden. One can find people who deal unjustly, violate God's command and legal authority, and deceive people among all nations. This will be discussed and demonstrated at greater length below.

Leviticus 19 forbids dealing unjustly.

18

The *Schlangenbalg* writes further about our Talmud. However, he does not write where it is found, neither tractate nor page. This is what he says. The Jews say in their Talmud: "*One who guards his mouth and tongue before the uncircumcised;*[52] *he is worthy of the world to come.*" This means, whoever keeps his mouth closed and does not say anything before the obstructed Christians, who do not know about God, he is a child of the eternal life. *I say,* "*May the Lord cut off all flattering lips*" [Psalms 12:4]. One will not find this in any Talmud.

This is a verse from Proverbs 21:23, "*He who guards his mouth and tongue, guards himself from trouble.*" This means, whoever guards his mouth and tongue from evil speech, he guards his soul from suffering, since the tongue brings some people to fear and neediness. It is a common warning among all people; it refers to both Jew and Christian.

Proverbs 21.

The apostate writes a public lie against our Talmud, and adds uncircumcised ones to it, when he writes that we call the Christians "uncircumcised

Apostate writes that we call the Christians "uncircumcised." It will be answered below in chapter 4, paragraph 6.

51. *Hoshen Mishpat* is a section of the *Shulchan Aruch*, the code of Jewish law written by Rabbi Joseph Karo (1488–1575). *Maimuni* refers to the *Mishneh Torah*, the code of Jewish law compiled by Moses Maimonides (1135–1204).
52. A reference to Christians.

ones." He translates "uncircumcised ones" as obstructed ones who do not know God. This will be answered below in chapter 4, paragraph 6.

A Jew was tortured to death in 5342 because of a blood libel.

The apostate writes further, in the year 5342, that is, 1582 according to the Christian calendar, in Dietenheim, in Swabia, a Jew was tortured to death because he would not talk. Therefore, his whole family was highly regarded among us because he did not want to confess that he had killed the Christian child. Concerning this, I say that the poor Jew did not know what to say, because he was innocent in the matter. Instead, they pressed it out of him with the lumber. The poor Jew remained with the truth until his death; *he guarded his mouth and tongue*, here or there. The poor Jew remained with the truth until his death. However, we want to make amends to him and esteem him, as this is commanded by God: to have compassion and pity for widows and orphans, whether Jew or Christian, especially when somebody loses his life so tragically. It is no response to the above, and it will not help to draw upon the freedoms from his majesty, the emperor, and the pope, since we are, with God's help, innocent of these things.

19

The apostate writes further. When the Christians say to the Jews, "Why did your ancestors kill Yeshua of Nazareth?" we say together in our houses: "O that we do not want to forget the hanged one who was killed." There are so many killings that happen here and there in the world and are forgotten. I say this, though I might suffer, that it was forgotten, but I am often accused of it, and we cannot atone for this. Yeshua of Nazareth himself asked this of us, as is mentioned above.

20

Apostate says that Yeshua the Nazarene must crawl out of all the corners on Christmas night.

The apostate, *Schlangenbalg*, writes here: We Jews eat garlic on Christmas night to disgrace Yeshua the Nazarene, and he says a foolish thing, that we Jews say that he must crawl out of all the corners on this night. If we were to study Torah, then he would rest. Therefore we do not study but instead, play, eat, and drink to excess, etc.[53]

Why Jews eat garlic.

First, concerning garlic, I say that we have inherited this from our ancestors. They also gladly ate it, as in Numbers 11.

53. On the history of this belief, see Shapiro, "Torah Study on Christmas Eve."

"*We remember the fish, etc.*" [Numbers 11:5]. We remember the fish that we used to eat in Egypt, and the cucumbers, leeks, the onions, and garlic. The Germans do not have a taste for garlic; so they have made a discovery, that we eat it. It is the same when we have a holiday or when the Christians have a holiday, we do not come to the Christians or deal with them. It might happen that someone eats garlic on Christmas Eve, since the Christians celebrate for several days and do not deal with us. However, this is not because we want to do it because of Yeshua the Nazarene. Who would believe such foolishness?

Numbers 11.

It is clear that garlic is considered healthy to eat, according to our Talmud. *As they say, five things were said concerning garlic, etc.*[55] Garlic is healthy for five things. We Jews who wander and do not eat warm foods, and drink out of all pools; garlic is healthy for this.

Garlic is healthy.[54]

Johannes Buxtorf, professor in Basel, writes in his book, *Judenschul*, why we eat garlic. In Italy, France, and Spain, dukes and nobles, as well as ordinary people, eat garlic. However, this apostate was no closer to Jerusalem than four miles from Speyer, that is, Worms, as mentioned above. However, that we supposedly eat and drink to excess and make merry on Christmas Eve is a complete lie. On the contrary, we should mourn, since because of Yeshua the Nazarene who was born on this night, we are rejected and must suffer much. It can sometimes happen that *Hanukkah* should happen at the same time. We eat and drink then, but not because of the foolishness that the apostate said. Can the apostate, may his name be blotted out, not allow us the poor stinking garlic? He is supposed to have been a Jew. How much more so, now that he devours bloodwurst and pig's knuckles at the dawn of the day. "*Spider's poison is on their lips*" [Psalms 140:4]. "*He who breaches a stone wall will be bitten by a snake*" [Ecclesiastes 10:8]. Enough of the first chapter.

Johannes Buxtorf writes why Jews eat garlic in his book, *Judenschul*, p. 290 and p. 340.[56]

54. On the history of this topic, see Diemling, "As the Jews Like to Eat Garlick."
55. B. *Baba Kama* 82a.
56. This citation is accurate and is from the first edition (Basel, 1603).

CHAPTER 2

Herein the falsehoods that the apostate from Oettingen, Samael Friedrich Brenz, brought into print against the community of Israel will be refuted and answered.

1

The apostate *Schlangenbalg* writes in the beginning of his second chapter that we call Christ's mother a ritually impure prostitute. That is, an unclean whore. **Above, chapter 1, paragraph 1.**

In the beginning of my first chapter, I demonstrated that we do not disdain or curse Yeshua the Nazarene and his followers. We are also not taught this by our sages and sacred books. Where our Talmud writes about Jesus, it cannot mean the Yeshua the Nazarene whom the Christians believe in, as we have demonstrated above with ten testimonies.

However, it might be spoken mockingly by women and unlearned coarse people, which we do not tolerate or authorize. It could be against the Jesus who is mentioned in the Talmud. **Chapter 1, paragraph 6.**

So have we responded above, that *Tola* and *Tolea*[1] cannot be translated as "one worthy of hanging" or "evildoer." Its meaning is uncertain, as we have written above at length. **Chapter 1, paragraph 1.**

1. *Tolea* is the active form of hanged in Hebrew, while *Taluy* is the passive form.

2

The apostate writes further that we call their holiday: "*trefah hanged one's holiday.*" This is the unclean gallows festival. I say that this is also a piece of his stupidity and falsehoods, since the word *trefah* does not belong here. *Trefah* refers to *a living thing*; that is, about a living thing, like a domestic or wild animal or fowl, that has been torn apart by a wild animal or bird of prey.

Genesis 37.

As Jacob said in Genesis 37, "*My son's tunic, a savage beast devoured him, Joseph was torn by a beast*" [Genesis 37:33]. This is my son's shirt. A wild animal has torn him; Joseph has been devoured.

***Trefah* is not "unclean."**

Trefah is not "unclean"; rather *tameh* is "unclean." I want to bring a number of proofs from the Torah, Prophets, and Writings. I do not know how *trefah* comes into his mouth. I can only assume that he once heard that a Jew called another one a "*trefah* butcher." That is, someone who had an animal with a broken leg and was *trefah*, and he sold it as kosher. Thus the apostate wanted to use the word *trefah* in all of his lies, as he does below in many places where he writes *trefah* where it is not an accident or an affliction, as he writes below in many places, and as I will report, God willing.

Chapter 3, paragraph 15. The apostate makes himself a liar with the word trefah.

Particularly, in chapter 3, paragraph 15, the apostate makes himself a liar with his *trefah* mouth. *And they brought it according to the rules of trefah.* When one brings a cow to be examined and it fails, we say that the cow is *trefah*. This cannot mean "unclean" in translation. It was permitted according to the Torah. However, when *trefah* would be impure, one should not have eaten it, according to the Torah, as it is written, *Do not eat anything unclean.*[2] We also call the hindquarter *trefah*. When the veins are removed, then it is kosher. Thus *trefah* cannot mean "unclean."

Exodus 22 describes *trefah* as "to break."

See also how the *Targums* describe *trefah*, in Exodus 22. "*If it was torn by beasts*" [Exodus 22:12]. "*When it will be broken, etc.*"[3] This means, when it will be broken. In conclusion, *trefah* cannot be translated as "unclean."

The apostate writes further that we call the disciples of Yeshua the Nazarene "the *trefah* disciples of the hanged one." This means the unclean, extirpated disciples of the hanged one. The liar always cites *trefah*

2. A paraphrase of Judges 13:14.
3. *Targum Onkelos* on Exodus 22:12.

regarding this. In all of our holy books we only find "*disciples of the Nazarene.*" This means, in Yiddish, the disciples of the Nazarene. *Trefah* is not "unclean" anywhere. Therefore, his lies make no sense.

3

The apostate writes further that we call the holiday of the disciples of Yeshua the Nazarene "the *trefah disciples' festival.*" This means "the unclean, blotted-out, disciples' holiday." So I say that one should examine all the calendars and almanacs where we write about them and name them, the same way that Christians name them, Peter, Paulus, Jörg, Johannes, Jakob.[4]

4

The apostate writes that we call the Lutheran priests "unclean false teachers."

The apostate writes further that we call the Evangelical or Lutheran preachers "*trefah teachers of falsehood.*" This means "the unclean false teachers." I must laugh at his understanding of Hebrew here. The *trefah* character again translates *trefah* as "unclean." He is as quick in grammar as an elephant for jousting. Let somebody who understands better than I do translate *melamdonim* for me. Before God, Blessed be He, I can swear that I have never heard Lutheran preachers called by such a name other than Lutheran priests. However, the learned among us call them *darshanim*, which are preachers. When this apostate liar wants to rhyme his lies, he should write "*darshanim, shakranim, u-temai'im.*" This would have been, "the unclean, false preachers." However, *trefah melamdonim* goes together like a camel through the eye of a needle.[5] *I have written at length in the book for Christians*, about how the apostate is an ignoramus.

---

4. These are significant saints' days on the Christian calendar. Peter and Paul are the primary apostles, and their days are significant holy days. Jörg (Saint George) is celebrated on April 23; Johannes (John the Baptist) on June 24; Jakob (the Patriarch Jacob) on July 25. The last three dates are celebrated only by Catholics and have significance on German peasants' agricultural calendar, where they mark milestones in the growing season. My thanks to my friend Pfarrer Helmut Foth for this information.

   The early modern Jewish relationship with the Christian calendar is discussed in E. Carlebach, *Palaces of Time: Jewish Calendar and Culture in Early Modern Europe* (Cambridge, MA: Belknap Press of Harvard University Press, 2011), chapters 5 and 6.
5. An allusion to Matthew 19:24; Mark 10:25; Luke 18:25.

5

***Apifior* is an important name that comes from Latin.**

The apostate writes further that "pope," *pifior*, is a very contemptuous name. I say that it is shown in all books that it is a very esteemed name, like *noble*, *counselor*, duke, *apifior* (in the *Hanukkah* prayers). However, the truth is that the word comes from Latin, and in the Italian language the pope is called *Papi*. Thus we say *pafior* or *pifior*. The "ior" is a form of the language, as we say *spanior* or *gasconior*.

Zalman says *pifior* is two words.

However, I say that *pifior* is two words, like *piv yor*. That is, "his mouth teaches," because he is the chief among the Christians, and they follow his teachings. So it is not a defect according to grammar that one needs the *peh* instead of the *vav*. Take what is good in your eyes. However, it can never be shown that *apifior* is a contemptuous name. Many baptized Jews in Rome have thoroughly examined the prayers. They have found *apifior* many times in them and could not translate it as even one despicable name.

6

The *Schlangenbalg* writes further that we call a cardinal *kur dalfon*. I have never heard this in all my days. I also do not know what this is. I will swear that the apostate also does not know what he has written. All of our books call them *hasmona'im*. That is, ecclesiastical nobles.

Psalms 68.

As we find in Psalms 68, "*Tribute bearers* [*hashmanim*] *shall come from Egypt*" [Psalms 68:32]. The Maccabean priests called themselves "Hasmoneans," which means "priests." That is why we call the cardinals *hasmona'im* in Hebrew. However, ordinarily we call them "cardinals." See in the *Tishbi*, under the root *Hashman*.[6]

***Tishbi*, root *Hashman*.**

The *Schlangenbalg* writes that *Hegemon* is a despicable name. It is a name of greatness and honor in all books. It is found many times in the prayerbook. The Roman apostates did not strike it out.[7]

---

6. Eliyahu Bahur, *Sefer ha-Tishbi* (Isny, 1541), s.v. *Hashman*. This second part of this paragraph, including the reference to Psalms 68:32, comes from this source.

7. A reference to the Christian censors of Hebrew books and manuscripts who struck out or deleted words they thought were derogatory to Christianity.

See in tractate *Shabbat*;[8] also in the beginning of [tractate] *Gittin*;[9] also in [Midrash] *Tanhuma, Parshat Yitro*.[10] They all show that *Hegemon* is a name of greatness and honor.

Shabbat 145; beginning of Gittin; Tanhuma, Parshat Yitro.

However, the essence and truth is that *Hegemon* is a Greek word and means "a leader." It also means "a leader" in Hebrew.

Hegemon is a compound word, Heg Hamon.

In my opinion, it is a compound word, *Heg Hamon*. This means a leader of the ordinary people.

Rashi comments on "Ruler and Hegemon"[11] as nobles and hegemons.

Rashi comments on the words "Rulers and Hegemons": nobles and hegemons.

The Targum is "Leader and Hegemon."

The *Targum* comments: "leader and hegemon." Thus you see that it is an honest name, and the apostate is a liar.

8

The apostate writes that we call the cathedral[12] canons "*impure nobles*." This means "the unclean nobles." *The impure shall be called impure*. We do not call them anything other than "cathedral canons," "cathedral deacons," "cathedral deans."

9

He writes further that we call the Crusaders *trefah cross nobles*. The liar can say no more than *trefah* with regard to this. He translates it differently, which cannot be, as mentioned above.[13]

10

The apostate writes much rubbish. We call an abbot a "*priest*" [*comer*]; an abbess a "*priestess*" [*comerin*]; a nobleman a "*lunatic*" [*sahor*]; a noblewoman

8. B. *Shabbat* 145b.
9. B. *Gittin* 2a.
10. Midrash *Tanhuma, Yitro* 5.
11. B. *Shabbat* 145b.
12. The German word for cathedral is *Dom* or in earlier German, *Thum*, which sounds like the term for ritual impurity in Hebrew, *Tumah*.
13. See paragraph 2 in this chapter.

a "*female lunatic.*" The apostate says that these are noble-mocking names. I say that this ignorant apostate does not understand any of these words.

Comer* in Aramaic is "one who is locked in"; *comerin* is a "woman who is locked in."

Comer translates in Aramaic as "one who is locked in." *Comerin* is a "locked-in woman"; because they are locked into the cloister. See also *the priests of Pharaoh.* Therefore, we call the locked-in monks *comers* and other priests *galohim.*

Nobleman, freeman, like "the nobles of Judah."

We call a nobleman a *sahor.* This translates as a "free person," like "*the nobles of Judah*" [Jeremiah 27:20], the nobles and freemen of Judah. "*The nobles, the prefects*" [Nehemiah 4:8]. We find this mostly in Scripture. The grammarians call this the "imaginary *kaf.*" It is a form of the word. It could also be *kahor*, as in "baron," because the noble is somewhat lower than a baron. The Ashkenazi Jews mixed up the language. They substitute a *het* for a *heh* and say *kahor. I have discussed this at length in my book for the Christians.*

***Erubin* 139; *Hullin* 53.[14] *Kiri*, a master.[15]**

So too is *kiri* a "master" in the Arab language or Arabic. *Erubin* and *Hullin*, in Rashi's commentary there.

11

The *Schlangenbalg* says that we call a schoolmaster a *tulmaster*, and sometimes add *trefah* to it. I have not heard this said.

***Tul* means "a youth" in the language of the *Targum*.**

However, the one who says it derives from the Chaldean language, which calls youths *tul.* Thus when I say *tulmaster*, I mean the master of the youths.

12

The apostate further writes that we call a town clerk or a magistrate's clerk a *kofer.* This means in Yiddish "one who denies God." *Kofer* is found often in the Torah, Prophets, and Writings. However, in Yiddish it means "a redemptive exchange." The Christians translate it as "atonement"; that is "peace," as in Exodus 30.

---

14. There is a printer's mistake here. It is actually B. *Erubin* 53b and B. *Hullin* 139b.

15. The phrase "*Kiri*, a master," is from Rashi's commentary.

"Each shall pay a ransom for his soul" [Exodus 30:12]. A man should give the redemption or atonement for his soul. That is, he gives the money instead of his soul. According to the apostate's words, it would be a very negative statement, heaven forbid. Also, "*if ransom is laid upon him*" [Exodus 21:30].

Exodus 30.

The procurator and the advocates who we call the representatives are called "proper *koferim*," as they fulfill the word because of their principles and impartiality. He stands by it, speaks for it, and resolves the matter with justice and peace. Therefore he is called "a reconciler and deliverer." This is *kofer* in Hebrew, from the verse in Job 33.

We call the procurator and the advocates "a proper *kofer*."

"*If he has a representative, one advocate against a thousand to declare the man's uprightness: Then He has mercy on him and decrees, redeem him from descending to the Pit, for I have obtained his ransom*" [Job 33:23–24]. This means, if somebody has an angel or a herald who carries his merits before him, he will be pardoned and saved from Gehenna, and find forgiveness or redemption. The verse modestly calls him "an advocate for ransom."

Job 33.

Therefore we call every pious procurator and representative *kofer*. That is, "a redeemer." However, we call ordinary clerks "scribe" or "scribes." However, some women and unlearned men do not know the difference and call all clerks *kofer*. This is "redeemer," but not a denier of God, as the poisonous *Schlangenbalg* writes.

The verse calls him "an advocate for ransom." Job 33.

13

The apostate writes that we call the Catholic or popish religion "the old *evil religion*." This means "the old evil belief."

14

We call the Evangelical or Lutheran religion the "new *evil religion*." This means "the new evil belief." No honest person can say that we add the word *evil* or bad.

15

The apostate lies further and writes that we call the Calvinists "heretics," and that they are unbelievers. Why should we call the Calvinists greater heretics than the others who falsely believe in a blind faith? Yet they still believe in God in heaven.

The apostate says in chapter 7 that we call the Jews who do not believe in the Talmud "heretics."

See who the heretics are from the root of the word *heretic*. The prayer against heretics was enacted in the time of Ezra, before there were any Christians or Calvinists on the earth. The chronicles write that there was someone called Mani, and he said that there were two gods. One god works and does everything good; the other god, everything evil, and [he] was the one in whom Mani believed.

The name was given for Mani, their teacher and master.

These were called *Min* [Manicheans], after their heretical master who led them astray. Thus it is also true that the word *min* means "one who mixes up two species or varieties."[16]

Christians are not *Minim*.

However, no Christian is a *min*, as I will write further.

16

The apostate writes that we call the Latin language "an impure language." That is, an unclean language. Latin is not unclean for me. Rashi, of blessed memory, mentions in the Talmud, "*Latin is a distinguished language that is utilized by kings*."[17]

Latin is a beautiful language.

Latin is an exceptional language that is utilized by kings. We call it *lashon Romi*, the Roman language, in all of our books. Our *Sanhedrin*, Talmudic sages, Rashi, and Maimonides all studied Latin. We are allowed to pray in Latin. The word *oreh* is a Latin word that means "to pray" in Yiddish.[18] How then should the language be unclean? All languages come from God, Blessed be He. However, Hebrew is called "a holy language." This is the holy language, since God, Blessed be He, and the angels speak this language, and the Torah was given with it.

---

16. The confusion of the word *min*—which can mean either "variety" or "species" but in other contexts also is a term for "heretic"—is a common trope in this period. Censors often assumed that all uses of *min* meant "heretic" and often substituted *apikores* (Epicurean) as a more acceptable term.
17. I found this phrase used in B. *Avodah Zarah* 10a, *Tosafot*, but not in Rashi. The reference there is to Greek, not Latin.
18. *Oren* is a Western European Yiddish word for praying. The Latin *oreh* evolved into *oren* in German Yiddish. The better-known Eastern European Yiddish equivalent word is *davenen*.

So we call all other languages, in comparison to it, "secular," a non-holy language, but not "the unclean language." Why would Latin be an unclean language in comparison to German or Turkish? See Deuteronomy 27. "*And on those stones you shall inscribe every word of this teaching most distinctly*" [Deuteronomy 27:8]. Concerning this, our sages, of blessed memory, said that one must inscribe the Torah in all languages.[19] Latin was not the easiest among them. In Italy they call Latin from time to time *lashon tumo*, with a *vav* at the end [of the word]. This is because it is the church language, since it is used in the churches. However, not as the apostate writes, *tame* [impure], with an *aleph* at the end [of the word].

All languages are called "secular languages" in comparison to Hebrew.

17

Some people call Latin *lashon dima*, that is, "a mixed language," because it is no longer pure, and is mixed with Italian. *I have discussed this at length in the book that I have prepared for the Christians.*

Latin is a mixed language.

18

The *Schlangenbalg* writes further that we deliberately use Christian writings, and especially where Yeshua the Nazarene is written or printed, to clean ourselves in the toilet. This is a lie and a falsehood. We do not do this deliberately. Our books and sages do not tell us to do this.

The apostate writes that we use their writings and books for the toilet.

19

The apostate writes that we call a church "an abomination" [*toevah*]. This means "useless" and "abomination" in Yiddish. I say that the ignoramus has confused the word. We also call our synagogue a *tevah*. *He who descends before the tevah to pray*. This means the one who goes to the reader's stand to pray.

We call a reader's stand or lectern on which one prays a *tevah*. So we may also say about their churches, "*tevah*." However, not with the *ayin*.[20] Anthonius Margaritha, an apostate, writes the same in his book. However, in truth the ordinary person calls their churches *bet tefilatam*. This means "their houses of worship."

The reader's stand on which one prays is called *tevah*.

19. M. *Sotah* 7.5.

20. Adding an *ayin* to *tevah* (reader's stand) makes *toevah* (abomination).

20

Why we sometimes call the church *duomo*.

However, concerning that which the apostate writes that we call a church "*house of the cross or residence*." It is false that we sometimes call it *tumo* [impure].

This comes from the Christians, because they also call it this, from the Latin *duomo*, which means "palace" or "residence." However, the apostate wants to make *tumah* [impurity] out of it. I did not know this before; who knows about false tongues [languages]?

21

The apostate writes further that when we see Christian children being baptized, we say, "*mamzer shmad*" [an apostatized bastard]. This means "the child of a whore that is being destroyed." We call the Christian children *mamzers* because they are children of whores. Concerning this, I say and prove that Christians are not the children of whores, and we do not consider them to be so.

***Yevamot*, page 44, says that no child is a *mamzer* unless it is born of the adulterous relationship of a married woman.**

See *Yevamot* 44, where it is written that a child is not called a *mamzer* unless it is born of an adulterous relationship, or from a sexual relationship that is forbidden by the Torah, and one that is punishable by the death penalty.[21] So the Christians cannot be *mamzers*, since the Talmud says in *Sanhedrin*, "*The nations that are idol-worshipers gave no license to their women*."[22] That is, the nations that worship idols also do not make their wives vulgar, and therefore their wives are not whores, and their children are not the children of whores.

Christians are strict in their observance of the laws against adultery and illicit sexual relations. Therefore they are not *mamzers*.

How can we go against our Talmud to consider the children of the Christians to be the children of whores? They punish those who engage in adultery. The Christians forbid more forms of sexual relations than what the Torah had forbidden. It may be an easy friendship, but it should not lead to intermarriage. On the other hand, when a Christian man or woman converts and becomes a Jew, then we may marry them. If we consider them to be *mamzers*, then we could never marry them.

Deuteronomy 23.

As Deuteronomy 23 says, "*No mamzer shall be admitted into the congregation of the Lord, etc.*" [Deuteronomy 23:3].

21. B. *Yevamot* 44a.
22. B. *Sanhedrin* 82a.

They are not *mamzers*, but all nations who are not Jews are called a *foreign nation*. This means from a foreign nation. The apostate shows this in the worst light for us. It sometimes happens that when someone says this quickly, he *drops the ayin* so that one thinks that he said *mamzer*.[23] However, this cannot mean the Christian. Scripture also calls us *mamzer*.

All nations are called *from a foreign nation*.

Zechariah 9, "*And a mamzer shall settle in Ashdod*" [Zechariah 9:6]. The *Targum* says about this, "*Israel will dwell in Ashdod and will be like strangers*."[24] This means Israel will dwell in Ashdod and will be treated like strangers. So, see that the word *mamzer* translates as "stranger" and not as "children of whores." The apostate is an ignoramus. The *patakh* causes the transformation of an *aleph* or an *ayin*, *as is known to the grammarians*.

Zechariah 9. "And a mamzer shall settle in Ashdod."

22

The apostate writes again *inappropriately*, that when they have the call for the morning and evening prayers, the Jews say that one calls with the *trefah toleha* bell. This means, the "unclean gallows bell." So how does *trefah* become a bell, or why is the prayer bell for morning and evening more of a *trefah toleha* bell than when one calls on Friday afternoon? You have often heard above the meaning of *taluy* or *toleha*. It cannot be understood as "a gallows" or "unclean." There is nothing wrong with prayer. One calls for it or one knocks, as we Jews do.[25] *His son the apostate testifies falsely*.[26] No sensible Jew does this.

23

The apostate writes that we call a *kelch* [chalice] in the church *kelev*. This means a dog. I say, what does a dog have to do with a goblet? This is not an understandable lie. He heard people say, but he did not know where, that we call our holy vessels *kelav*. This is "vessels" and does not mean "dog."

The apostate writes that we call a *kelch* [chalice], a *kelev*; that is, a dog.

We find in Exodus 25, with regard to the Tabernacle, "*the pattern of all its furnishings, etc.*" [Exodus 25:9]. That is, the pattern of the Tabernacle, and

Exodus 25

23. Spoken quickly, "*me-am zar*" ("from a foreign nation") can sound like *mamzer*.
24. *Targum* to Zechariah 9:6.
25. Rather than ringing a bell as Christians did, the synagogue beadle would go around the Jewish quarter and knock on the window or door with a small hammer to announce the time for morning prayers.
26. A paraphrase of Deuteronomy 19:18.

all of its vessels. I want to believe the opposite, that the Christians took the word *kelch* from our language, the *Holy Tongue* [Hebrew], from *keilecha*, which is "vessels." Thus *kelav* and *keilecha* have one root. One does not write it with a *bet* at the end.[27]

24

The apostate writes that we call the mass vestments [*messgewand*] *mita gewand*. That is, "death vestments." What pushes the donkey to falsehood? He should have left it at "*mes* vestment." This does translate as "death vestment." How should we call it anything else when the Christians themselves call it this? Often there is a word in one language that means the opposite in another language. This is nothing new. In German, "cold" [*kalt*] is called *frisch* [fresh, cool]. In Italian, "cold" [*caldo*] is called "warm." We also do not call it anything other than *messgewand*.

25

Reason for *water of impurity*.

The apostate writes that we call the holy water in the baptismal font *water of impurity*. This means the "unclean waters," in Yiddish. The apostate does not understand the reason. If he had studied the Pentateuch first, he would have understood it better.

Numbers 19.

See Numbers 19. "*Anyone who touches a person who was killed, or human bone, or a grave*" [Numbers 19:16]. "*A person who is clean shall take hyssop, dip it in the water, and sprinkle, etc.*" [Numbers 19:18]. "*The clean person shall sprinkle it on the unclean person, etc.*" [Numbers 19:19]. "*The water of lustration was not dashed on him, etc.*" [Numbers 19:20]. "*He who sprinkled the water of lustration . . . whoever touches the water of lustration*" [Numbers 19:21]. There are so many [examples] that our water in the Tabernacle or Temple was also called *water of impurity*. We sprinkled the unclean and the leprous and purified them.

Jews also called their water *water of menstruation and water of impurity*.

Therefore we called them "water of menstruation and water of impurity." This means "the unclean water." (That is, water that was needed for the unclean ones.) However, the substance or essence of the word is not unclean.

27. The word *kelav* (vessels) is spelled differently from *kelev* (dog), though they sound similar when spoken.

Since the papacy, from ancient times to the present, they sprinkle the graves and the people with the water without distinction. They also baptize the children with it. They are purifying them from Adam's sin, as they say themselves. Thus it is correctly called *waters of impurity*. That is, water of the unclean. One sprinkles the unclean with it. However, the water is not unclean. If it were, our water in the Temple and the Tabernacle would also have been unclean.

See in the Gospels of Matthew, Mark, Luke, that Yeshua, their messiah, himself told the lepers and the unclean ones to go to the *cohen* or priest, to have themselves sprinkled and cleansed.[28] In conclusion, the apostate does not know the Torah, much less his Gospels.

Matthew 8, Mark 1, Luke 5.

26

The ignorant apostate comes once again. We pray every Sabbath for the Jews who interfere with baptism. He heard being read in the memorial book, "*for the sake of those who stopped the destruction and stopped the taxes, etc.*" This is in Yiddish, "for the sake of those who stopped the evil decrees of death and the taxes."

All the books translate *shmadot* as "destructions" but not "baptisms."

Shmad **is translated as "destruction" but not "baptism."**

Let the apostate translate "*destroy* [*le-hashmid*], *massacre, and exterminate, etc.*" [Esther 3:13, 7:4]. Here, there was no baptism on the earth.[29] Martin Luther and all the Christian scholars translate *shmad* as "destruction." Does he want to translate *shmad* as "baptism"? Does he want to cross swords with them?

Book of Esther.

It is written in Psalms 37. "*But transgressors shall be utterly destroyed*" [Psalms 37:38].

Psalms 37.

"*But all the wicked He will destroy*" [Psalms 145:20]. It is enough for the wise. There are many more examples.

Psalms 145.

28. Matthew 8:4; Mark 1:44; Luke 5:14.
29. That is, the events in the Book of Esther occurred long before the founding of Christianity.

27

Why the relatives of apostates are scorned.

The *Schlangenbalg* writes further that when one of us allows himself to be baptized, his whole family is held in low esteem. True, the reason will become clear when I respond to the apostates. This is because the majority of times they have themselves baptized because of evil deeds and not because of faith. Afterward, they tell and write all kinds of lies and intrigues about us, out of hatred. Then the family is scorned, and it is cast before them. *I have expanded on these matters in the book that I have written for the Christians.*

28

The apostate writes that we call the consecration of a church *kirdol.* I say that I do not know what *kirdol* is, and have never heard it. This term is not used in any of the languages that I am familiar with.[30]

29

We call a baptized Jew *meshumad.*

The apostate writes that we call a baptized Jew a *meshumad.* This means "one who has been blotted out by God." Concerning this, I say and will prove that the word *meshumad* is "someone who is estranged." That is someone who makes himself a stranger, does not want to make known who he is. He could equally be a Jew, a Christian, or a Turk. When someone changes his religion and does not want to be what he was born, he is called a *meshumad,* "one who is estranged."

Ramban on the verse, "*No foreigner shall eat of it.*"

As Ramban writes concerning the verse, "*No stranger shall eat of it*" [Exodus 12:43]. One who changes his faith is called a *meshumad.* He takes the language from the *Targum,*[31] from the phrase, "*Joseph made himself a stranger to his brothers*" [Genesis, 42:7]. See for yourself that a Jew or a gentile is called a *meshumad* when he changes or mixes up his deeds.[32] As our sages write everywhere, when someone transgresses a commandment of the Torah, like eating pork or something similar, they write that he is a *meshumad for eating pork.* That is to say, one who is estranged makes himself a stranger and eats pork, as if he did not know that the Torah had forbidden it. Therefore, it is not unjust, and much more so one is called a

30. This may be a variation of the German term *Kirchtag* (*Kirtog* in dialect). My thanks to the anonymous reviewer for this suggestion.

31. *Targum Onkelos* to Genesis, 42:7.

32. Ramban to Exodus 12:43.

meshumad when he transgresses the whole Torah. One who is born a Jew sealed the bargain at Mount Sinai.[33] It is written,

"*Not with you alone, etc.*" [Deuteronomy 29:13]. This means, not with you alone did I establish this covenant and oath, but with those who were present on this day to hear our God, and with those who were not here, etc. Therefore, no Jew can extract himself from this oath. We all swore to keep the Torah. Whoever does not do this, and transgresses much or little of it, is called a *meshumad*, one who is estranged. That is to say, one who wants to say, "I am a stranger, and I was not there when the Torah was given." For this reason we do not call any Christian a *meshumad*, since he did not receive the Torah or take it upon himself and is not obligated to keep it.

Deuteronomy 29. All Jews swore to keep the Torah, even those who were not personally at Mount Sinai.

30

An apostate, Anthonius Margaritha, writes that he can completely tolerate that he is called a *meshumat*. In translation this is "one who has escaped." One who has escaped from a severe judgment. This *meshumat* is with a *tet* at the end of the word. I am also satisfied with someone who allows himself to be called this. However, most of the time we call the baptized Jews "apostates" [*mumarim*]. This means they exchange things. That is, they exchange the laws and the Torah. This is how I, Zalman Zvi, translated the word *meshumad*. This will become clear in the place where I explain the phrase "and to the *meshumadim*."[34]

The apostate Anthonius Margaritha of Regensburg gladly allows himself to be called *meshumat*.

The apostate further writes that we give the Christian Eucharist many derisive names. I say that I have never heard this. It is forbidden to us, as is mentioned above in the first chapter. See how the falsehoods cannot make sense. He says that when a Christian goes to the Eucharist, the Jew says, "*You were made impure* [*metameh hayita*]." Let an expert in the Hebrew language tell me what this is. However, when a Jew supposedly says, "The Christian has eaten the hanged one," as the apostate writes, this is no insult. Many say this, as when the Jew says, "The Christian has eaten Yeshua the Nazarene."

The apostate writes that we give their Eucharist many derisive names.

Why Yeshua the Nazarene is called "the hanged one" can be found in the first chapter.

Why their messiah is called "the hanged one" is found above, in chapter 1. However, concerning that which the apostate writes, that we call the

33. He uses a German expression that literally means "drank the glass of wine that seals the bargain."
34. See *Theriak* 5.14.

Eucharist "an impure meal," that is, the unclean meal, this is an outright lie. This apostate will find how once, in a disputation between an apostate and a Jew in Rome, which was held before the pope, this was also thrown before the Jew, that the Roman Jews called the Eucharist *bread of blood.*

Why was their Eucharist called *bread of blood* for many years by the Roman Jews?

The Jew responded, because it is explicitly written in the Gospels of Matthew, Mark, and Luke, that Yeshua the Nazarene gave his disciples bread and wine at the Last Supper in Jerusalem, and said: "These were his body and his blood." They should do this in his memory.[35]

Matthew 26, Mark 14, Luke 23.

The Christians confess and believe that this is the body and blood of Yeshua, their messiah. The understanding is mixed up. It cannot be called in Hebrew more briefly or clearly than *bread of blood* (not with the *tet* as the apostate writes).[36] This is the food, the blood and the body. Everything is understood in the expression *demah*. I will leave it at this. However, I have not heard it called this.

31

The apostate writes that we spit on the cross and call it idol worship. This cannot be true. All Jews know that Christians do not consider the cross to be a god and do not worship it. They only consider it to be a reminder.

Jewish legal decisors write that gentiles are not idol-worshipers.

All of our legal decisors write: "*Gentiles in the present time are not idol-worshipers.*" The Christians are not idolaters. I will show you eleven testimonies from the Talmud that the Christians are not idolaters, and we do not consider them such. Where it is written "gentiles" in the Talmud it does not mean Christians, but the idolatrous nations, since the Talmud was composed in Babylonia in the time of the emperor Constantine. At that time the Christian religion was not yet dominant.

Testimony 1.

It is written in the Talmud, tractate *Avodah Zarah*, page 1. "*It is forbidden to have business dealings with the gentiles three days before their holidays, etc.*"[37] This means, three days before the gentile holidays, one should not do business with them, not lend them anything or any

35. Matthew 26:26–28; Mark 14:22–24; Luke 22:19–20.

36. The spelling of "impure" (*tumah*) in Hebrew is similar to "blood" in Aramaic (*demah*). The only difference is the first letter: *tet* in the first case and *dalet* in the second.

37. M. *Avodah Zarah* 1.1.

money or accept anything from them. However, we deal with the Christians before or after their holidays, even on the holidays, if they so desire.

One is not supposed to sell them cattle.[38] We daily sell them all kinds of **Testimony 2.**
cattle, only if they want to buy them.

One is not supposed to sell weapons to the gentiles, since they commit **Testimony 3.**
murder with them, and you tolerate it.

We sell the Christians all sorts of weapons. They punish the murderers with the wheel and dispense good justice.

One should not shelter cattle at gentile barns, since they engage in **Testimony 4.**
bestiality.[39]

We shelter all sorts of cattle in Christian barns and do not worry about that. They also burn such adulterers and pederasts, in accord with the laws of the Torah.

One should not trust any gentile and go across a field alone with him. **Testimony 5.**

When we Jews want to travel securely, we take along a Christian as an escort.

One should not utilize Christian physicians. They poison the Jews. **Testimony 6.**

Yet it is known that we utilize Christian physicians every day and do not worry about this.

Nobody should have their barbering needs fulfilled or their hair trimmed **Testimony 7.**
by the gentiles, since they are murderers, and they might cut your throat with the razor.[40]

We have no other barbers than Christians in all German and Italian lands where I have been. Also in Poland, and they do not worry about having their throats cut.

---

38. M. *Avodah Zarah* 1.6.
39. M. *Avodah Zarah* 2.1.
40. M. *Avodah Zarah* 2.2.

Testimony 8. We should not deal in Christian wine or have any benefit from it.[41]

Yet Jews in all lands deal with Christians in wine.

Testimony 9. You should have no benefit or pleasure from the gentile idols. If you receive one, you must grind it up and cast it to the wind or throw it into the sea.[42]

However, the Jews deal with coral and the paternoster objects, crosses, and the image of Yeshua the Nazarene. We buy them and resell them. If we would have considered the cross an idol, as the apostate writes, then we would have had to grind it up and throw it into the water.

Testimony 10. One should not pay customs duties or income taxes, because they belong to the gentile monasteries and wind up honoring their idols.

We give the Christians customs duties and income taxes to the monastery, which is a spiritual place.

Testimony 11. In [tractate] *Sanhedrin*, p. 63[b]. No Jew should associate with the gentiles. The gentile might lie to you, and so you might accuse him before the authorities. He is told to take an oath, and he swears by his idol.

***Sanhedrin*, p. 63.**

Exodus 23. It is written in the Torah, Exodus 23. "*Be on guard concerning all that I have told you. Make no mention of the names of other gods; they shall not be heard on your lips*" [Exodus 23:13]. This means, "You should keep everything that I have told you, and you should not mention the names of the idols, and they should not be mentioned because of you." However, we have all sorts of association with Christians. We also accept their oaths, and they swear by God Almighty and not by idols. *I have written at greater length in the book that I have made for the Christians.* So, I have shown with trustworthy witnesses that we do not consider Christians to be idol-worshipers, like the gentiles who are found in the Talmud. He cannot mean Christians with this but rather idol-worshipers who are heathens.

Why we call the Christians *goyim*. What is the reason that we call Christians *goyim*?[43] Is the reason that we do not know from what nation they are? The *Mikhlol*[44] writes in his introduction to part 2, see there, that we cannot give them a personal name.

41. M. *Avodah Zarah* 2.3.
42. M. *Avodah Zarah* 3.3.

Therefore we call them *goy*. This means a "nation," as Scripture also calls us Jews a *goy*.

Jews are also called *goyim*.

If we are pious, we are a holy *goy*. If, heaven forbid, we are evil, then we are called a sinful *goy*. Nobody should be ashamed of the word *goy*.

The apostate writes further that when we see a pile of sticks or a haystack in the shape of a cross, we quickly spit on them. It has often been mentioned above that the Torah said,

"*But for your own life-blood, etc.*" [Genesis 9:5]. How should we put ourselves in such danger, since our Torah has not commanded this? What does a cross of straw bother me? Why should I curse or despise it, as the apostate writes? Has the apostate done his? If he did this when he was a Jew, he acted as an ignoramus. *I have written at length in the book for the Christians*, that the apostate is lying.

Genesis 9.

32

The apostate writes further. When a Jew walks through a churchyard where there are graves, the Jews say that his prayers are not heard before God for thirty days. This is written in the Talmud, in [tractate] *Avodah Zarah*. I say that this is an outright lie.

In tractate *Ta'anit*, page 16. When one prays for rain, this is when one wants to ask God that He should allow the rain to fall, one should go to cemeteries to pray.

Ta'anit 16.

Where there are no Jewish cemeteries, we should go to gentile cemeteries.[45] On the other hand, on the eve of *Rosh Hashanah* and the eve of *Yom Kippur*, we go to the cemetery to pray. When there is no Jewish cemetery, we go to gentile cemeteries. If it were as the apostate writes, that our prayers are not heard for thirty days when we go to gentile cemeteries, how could we go to gentile cemeteries in the holy season? Tomorrow is

They go to gentile cemeteries to pray for rain.

---

43. The term *goy* (pl. *goyim*) in its original meaning is "nation." However, over the centuries it has come to mean non-Jew or gentile. Thus in this section I have not translated the term but rather allowed the author to explain it in his own way.
44. An important medieval work on Hebrew grammar by R. David Kimhi.
45. B. *Ta'anit* 16a.

Rosh Hashanah. Tomorrow is *Yom Kippur*, when we pray more than the rest of the year, if our prayers were not accepted for thirty days, heaven forbid? Everything that comes out of the mouth of the apostate is a lie, false and irrelevant. This will certainly demonstrate that we may pray at Christian cemeteries.

33

The *Schlangenbalg* writes further. When a Jew hears a Christian swear by the sacraments, the Jew says the gentile has sworn by the *sheger dumah*. This means he swore by the false and unclean religion. Here one sees his ignorance. He wanted to write *sheker tumah*, so he writes *shigur dumah*. I have not heard, but according to the words of the apostate himself, when someone says *shigur demah*, it is as if someone said "sent blood," since *sheger* means "sending"; *demah* means "blood." This is nothing shameful or negative, as the apostate writes.

34

The apostate writes that we ask God to ruin and destroy the Christian churches.

The apostate writes further. The Talmud commands that when we see a ruined church, we should praise God that He ruined it, and wish that all churches should be ruined in this way. It is written clearly and lucidly there. When one sees a house of idol worship, this is an idol's house.[46] However, when one sees a Christian church, we do not consider it a house of idol worship, as written above. Sufficient answers for the second chapter.

---

46. B. *Avodah Zarah* 46a.

CHAPTER 3

Herein will be shown that we hold the rulers in great honor and we pray for them, and that it is forbidden for us to deceive Christians or to swear falsely against them. Similarly, the false words and curses, and even more so murder, are forbidden in the Written and Oral Torah, and it is never permitted to do any evil to Christians.

1

The apostate writes in this book called *Schlangenbalg* that we Jews publicly (that is, in public) appear to be obedient to the rulers. However, in our hearts and secretly, we curse and execrate them. Concerning this, I say that *it is an outright lie.* We are obedient and faithful to the emperor, king, and rulers.

The apostate writes that the Jews curse the rulers secretly.

Whoever curses his rulers acts against God, who has put the ruler in his place, *since He is the one who makes kings rulers.* When they are not gracious to us, this is because of our sins, and the Lord, Blessed be He, commanded the kings and rulers to do this, as Solomon said,

Whoever curses his ruler acts against the Holy One.

"*The mind of the king in the Lord's hand, etc.*" [Proverbs 21:1]. The king's heart is in God's hand. He leads him where he desires.

Proverbs 21.

The ruler is God's servant. Jeremiah the prophet called the idolatrous heathens "God's servants" (he said, "*Nebuchadnezzar My servant*" [Jeremiah 43:10]). Why should we, heaven forbid, curse the Christian emperor, king, or duke in our heart? They believe in God, as mentioned above. How should I secretly curse the king? Do I not know what Solomon said?

A king is called "God's servant."

Ecclesiastes.

"Don't revile a king even among your intimates" [Ecclesiastes 10:20]. Also, do not curse the king in your thoughts and do not execrate the rich in your bedroom, since the bird under heaven (these are God's angels) brings the cry, and that which has wings tells the matter. How should I hide the cursing from God? I must fear the punishment of God and of the king, and dare not object to His works.

Even if there were no Christian in the world, the Messiah would not come before the Holy One would want it to happen.

God desires that we should be dispersed in the exile. We would rather be under the Christian emperor or king than under the Turk or heathen. If I could curse all the Christians at one time, and it is not God's will to redeem us, then God would send someone on our necks who would be more ungracious than the Christians are to us. Our exile would not end with this. We are too weak to fight with God. Thus, see that it is contrary to reason to curse the rulers.

Zalman demonstrates from all books that gentiles and Jews should not curse the emperor and king.

I will demonstrate from many Christian books as well as from our books that we should not curse king, emperor, and nobles but should pray for their long lives.

1.1

That one should pray for emperor and king.

Jeremiah 29

See, Jeremiah the prophet writes to the Jews about going to Babylon, where they had been exiled. "*Seek the welfare of the city, etc.*" [Jeremiah 29:10]. Think about the welfare of the city to which I have exiled you. Pray for it to God, since when things go well for it, you will also benefit from it. Jeremiah wrote this at God's command.

1.2

***Chapters of the Fathers* 3.**

It is written in *Chapters of the Fathers*, "*Pray for the peace of the rulers, etc.*"[1] Pray for the peace and welfare of the king.

1.3

***Song of Songs Rabbah*, chapter 2; Two Judges of Decrees.**

Song of Songs Rabbah, chapter 2; Two Judges of Decrees.[2] Concerning the verse, "*I adjure you, O maidens of Jerusalem, by gazelles, etc.*" [Song of Songs 2:7]. *The Holy One adjured Israel with six oaths, etc. One of them was that they should not rebel against their rulers.* This means Israel swore six oaths

---

1. M. *Avot* 3.2.
2. *Song of Songs Rabbah* 2.1[7]; B. *Ketubot* 111a.

to the Holy One. One of them was that we would not rebel or do anything against the kings and governments of the nations where we dwell.

1.4

Yalkut, Kings 18 writes.[3] "*The Holy One commanded that one should honor kings, even if they are not worthy, like Pharaoh and Ahab, etc.*" God commanded that we should show respect to all the kings of the nations, even if they do not rule properly, like the rule of Pharaoh, king of Egypt, and Ahab, king of Israel.

***Yalkut*, Kings 18.**

1.5

Solomon said in his wisdom, "Fear the Lord, my son, and the king, and do not mix with dissenters" [Proverbs 24:21]. This means, "My son, fear God and the king. Do not mix with those who do otherwise, or hide and obligate yourself to them."

Proverbs 24.

1.6

The *Zohar* writes that the Torah commanded that seventy bulls be offered in Jerusalem for the seventy nations of the world, so that it should go well for them.[4] Other books also write this.

***Zohar* and other books.**

1.7

Josephus, whom the Christians call Josephus, writes in the long [book] *The Romans*, and many rely on it. He writes against someone called Apion, who wrote many falsehoods about how they curse kings. So Josephus writes on the meaning of the verse, "*You shall not revile God, etc.*" [Exodus 22:27], that you should also not curse or denigrate other nations.

Josephus to *The Romans*, page 851, in the book that he wrote against Apion.

Josephus cites many other similar proofs in chapter 8, page 98.

Josephus to *The Romans*, chapter 8, page 98.

1.8

It is written in the Book of Baruch that the Christians included in their Bible that the Babylonian Jews in their exile took money and sent it to

Book of Baruch. Jews took money from gentiles and sent it to Jerusalem to purchase sacrifices and spices for them.

3. *Yalkut Shimoni*, 1 Kings, *Remez* 217.
4. *Zohar* I: 261a.

Jerusalem, and included the following message with it: "We are sending you this money so that you should purchase sacrifices and spices for the incense that is burned in the Temple. You should pray for the health of Nebuchadnezzar, king of Babylon, and for the health of his son Belshazzar, that they should live long and they should be gracious to us, etc."[5]

1.9

Ezra 6. King Darius gave the Jews money. He commanded them to offer sacrifices and to pray for him.

King Darius found a letter that his predecessor, King Cyrus, had written, and he again confirmed it and fulfilled it. It read, "*out of the resources of the king, etc.*" [Ezra 6:8]. You should give the Jews money daily, from the king's income and authority, so that they should buy sacrifices to offer to God in heaven. They should pray for the king's long life and that of his children, etc.[6] They followed this faithfully.

Josephus to *The Romans*, book 11, chapter 4.

Josephus to *The Romans* also writes this in book 11, in chapter 4.

1.10

Tractate *Yoma*, chapter 7

In tractate *Yoma*, chapter 7, and the *Fasting Scroll* [*Megillat Ta'anit*], chapter 9: One finds that the Samaritans wanted King Alexander to destroy the Temple. Simeon the Just went to the king and said: "Why do you allow yourself to be misled by these people, that you want to destroy this place? There, they pray daily for you and for your kingdom."[7]

1.11

***Book of Maccabees*, chapter 7. The Jews opened all the books for King Demetrius and demonstrated that they prayed for him.**

In the *Book of Maccabees*, which the Christians call *Maccabeorum* and include in their Bible, it is written in chapter 7 how King Demetrius sent his field commander, Nicanor, to destroy the Temple. The Jews laid all the books before his eyes [to prove] that they pray for him and offer sacrifices, etc.[8]

1.12

Josephus writes about the Hasmoneans.

Josephus also writes in the place where he writes about the Hasmoneans that the centurion Eliadoro came to destroy the Temple. Onias the priest

5. Baruch, 1:10–11.
6. Ezra 6:1–10.
7. B. *Yoma* 69a; *Megillat Ta'anit*, chapter 9.
8. 1 Maccabees 7:26–33.

went toward him and said that he had no reason to attack the Temple, since they prayed there daily for the king and his children.

1.13

Josephus, *The Jews*, writes in book 6, chapter 47,[9] that the Jews in Asia sent a present to Hyrcanus the priest and the lords of Judah, so that they would pray for Emperor Augustus and Marco Antonio[10] of Rome.

Josephus, *The Jews*, book 6, chapter 77.

1.14

Josephus, who wrote to the Romans, writes in book 2, chapter 9, how Petronio, the field commander of the emperor Gaius, wanted his [the emperor's] image to be put in the Temple, as a remembrance. The Jews said that he should be satisfied that they prayed for him and his welfare every day in the Temple.

Josephus, *The Romans*, book 2, chapter 9.

1.15

Josephus writes further in book 2 of *Against Apion* that the Jews commonly have in their custom to praise and to highly commend the emperor, the Roman empire, and people, and Jews offered sacrifices for the Romans in the Temple, etc.

Josephus writes further in *Against Apion*, book 2, that Jews pray for the Roman emperor.

1.16

He also writes thusly about the emperor *Abi Sibia* in book 8, chapter 2. I would bring another hundred proofs, but enough about this. Notice, *you the reader*, that we blessed and prayed for the nations who worshiped the stars and constellations, who were godless heathens, and we brought sacrifices on their behalf when the Temple still stood. We also had our own kings and nobles at that time, so we did not have to do it, yet we did it. How should we Jews, now in exile, curse and denigrate the Christians? They do good, guard, and protect us. They are also not heathens or idolaters. Rather, they believe in God in heaven. Therefore no understanding heart should or can believe that we curse the Christians, heaven forbid. It is known that we Jews in all lands recite a blessing for our rulers every Sabbath; those in Rome, for the pope; we Ashkenazim, Bohemians, and

Josephus to *The Romans*. Jews previously prayed in the Temple for the gentiles who were idolaters. How much more so, when we are now in exile, do we pray for the Christians who are not idol-worshipers. Jews in all lands recite the blessing for their kings.

9. Marginal note has 77 but main text has 47.
10. The names of the roman emperors are bold face in the original text.

Austrians, the beloved Holy Roman emperor, and all the dukes of the empire; those in Poland, their king, and so forth. Each community their specific ruler, as I have faithfully translated in the book that I have written for the Christians. How could we go against our own mouth, one time blessing and the other time cursing? Does the Blessed One allow us to play with and mislead Him?

Psalms 12.

Is it not written in Psalms 12, "*Men speak lies to one another; their speech is smooth; they talk with duplicity. May the Lord cut off all flattering lips*" [Psalms 12:3–4]? This is a curse against those who speak with a divided heart and have two tongues in their mouth. God will cut them all to pieces. Whoever wants to be cursed can speak with two tongues. We Jews do not do this or anything like it.

2

I have shown in chapter 5, paragraph 15, who becomes a wicked kingdom.

The *Schlangenbalg* further brings a pile of lies and babble about the rulers when they do not want to fulfill our desires. We call them a *wicked kingdom.* This means "the wanton kingdom," and we curse them. This is a lie and a falsehood. In chapter 5, paragraph 15, it is shown when we call a kingdom "wanton." One may laugh about what the apostate ignoramus writes. We say to the rulers who do not give us our way, "*and the wicked kingdom quickly 'deyeagor.*"[11] Let this be translated by one who can.

3

The apostate writes further that we call the Christian counselors or advisors *yohazim.*[12] This means in Yiddish "they should tear themselves apart and become disunited." First, I have proven that we do not curse the rulers, and it is forbidden to speak falsely. No Jew calls the counselors anything other than *yoazim*, and this means "advisors."

The apostate writes further that we give the rulers bribes and that they take them. Thus we wish them bad luck [*schlim-mazal*]. The bad idiots [literally, *behemoth*: "cattle"]; those are the rulers who take bribes from us.

11. This word is most probably a misspelling of *yeaker*, "be uprooted" or "be eradicated." The author is mocking his opponent's inability to spell the word properly.

12. This is a play on words. *Yoazim*, or "advisors," is deliberately misspoken as *yohazim*.

Our religious decisors have always written about how they do not take bribes and maintain good justice and laws.

See in the *Responsa* of Rabbi Jacob Weil, section 111 and section 147.[13] There he writes that the rulers are not suspected of taking bribes. They are also believed without taking an oath. See there. *I have elaborated on this in the book that I have prepared for the Christians. You will find information about it in chapter 7. Here is not the place to elaborate.*

***Responsa* of Rabbi Jacob Weil 111 and 147, that the rulers are not suspected of taking bribes.**

4

The apostate writes further that we curse the Christians with all sorts of curses, and especially epilepsy. It is heard that one should not curse anyone. A Jew often uses this curse against someone who bothered him, and also a father to his child. Unfortunately, cursing is found among all nations.

We Jews curse no Christian who has not done anything against us.

However, we do not curse any Christian who has not done anything against us. Below I will demonstrate that one should not curse any heathen or heretic, much less a Christian.

6[14]

The apostate writes that we call the Christians "Haman" and *tormenter of the Jews*. I give these titles to Samael Friedrich the apostate and others like him. However, we do not do this to any Christians.

7

The apostate writes further. We call the mayor of the city "the chief uncircumcised one" [*rosh irol*]. This means, the "head of the uncircumcised ones"; those who do not know God. The apostate says a lie and a falsehood. We call him the "head of the city" [*rosh irin*]. This is the head of the burghers or the people of the city. The apostate makes *irol* [uncircumcised] out of *irin* [city]. One laughs at his grammar. He wanted to say

13. Rabbi Jacob Weil (d. before 1456) was an important German halakhic authority. His *Responsa* were first published in Venice, in 1523, and reprinted several times over the course of the next century.

14. It is not clear why the paragraph numbering skips paragraph 5. Perhaps this was a printer's error.

Responsa of Rabbi Jacob Weil, section 111 and section 247, that the heads of the cities are honest people.

orel,[15] but he said *irol*. On the contrary, I show here that we call them by their proper names and write it so in all books.

See the *Responsa* of Rabbi Jacob Weil.

Now the apostate says that when Jews mention a Christian, they always add *kaparah* [expiation] and *trefah* [nonkosher]. It has already often been heard that this is a falsehood. *I have expanded on this matter in the book for the Christians.*

Apostate writes that Jews are allowed to swear falsely against Christians.

The apostate writes that we allow each other to swear falsely against Christians. He bungles several passages from the *Kol Nidre* that are laughable. *In the book for the Christians*, I have written at great length and presented many proofs that are needed. I will cite enough here to show that the apostate is lying. *Kol Nidre* is not about an oath that a Jew gives to another Jew or one that a Jew gives against a gentile. It relates only to vows that a person takes upon himself or herself with a vow [*neder*] or with an oath. As the verse says, "*If a man makes a vow to the Lord or takes an oath imposing an obligation on himself*" [Numbers 30:3]. When someone makes a vow to fast or something else, *Kol Nidre* helps for that. An expert individual can help him annul the vow. This is by a person who is a great Torah scholar, or through three ordinary individuals. See in any commentary on the *Mahzor* or in all religious decisors that *Kol Nidre* does not help for vows when someone relies on it and thinks about *Kol Nidre* before he makes the vow, and makes the vow afterward. Then he must keep it.

Kol Nidre does not annul an oath.

However, no person in the world can say that *Kol Nidre* annuls an oath. Otherwise, one Jew might swear falsely against another Jew. It is written that no Christian or Jew is excluded from this.

Nedarim 28.

See in [tractate] *Nedarim*, what the Tosafists write.[16]

15. With regard to people, the term means one who is not circumcised. The word also has a botanical meaning with regard to trees, but he is referring to people in this context.

16. B. *Nedarim* 28a, s.v., "*Ve-ha-Amar Shmuel.*"

You shall not take what belongs to a Christian or deceive him. When you have incurred a tax and the customs agent catches you and asks you, on your oath, "What do you have with you?" you should not swear falsely to him, even if you certainly know that he will illegally take everything from you, against all law. See, you should not swear falsely even to a thief and a heathen. How should Jews swear falsely against Christians who believe in God? When they ask you to take an oath legally and in court, is it not written, "*You shall not swear falsely by the name of the Lord, etc.*" [Exodus 20:7]?

Testimony 1, one should not swear falsely against Christians.

"*You shall not swear*" forbids against all peoples.

One should not take the name of the Lord and swear falsely. There is no difference between Jews and Christians.

Did not our ancestors keep their oaths?

Testimony 2.

The two spies and scouts who swore to Rahab the prostitute.[17]

Joshua 6.

Was it not written in the Torah, "*You shall not let a soul remain alive*" [Deuteronomy 20:16]? You shall not allow anyone of the seven nations to remain alive. Yet they allowed Rahab and her father's household to remain alive, because of the oath. Only these two men did this, and it was an order to the king and the nobles. Should we swear falsely against Christians, heaven forbid?

Deuteronomy 7 and 27.[18]

Take an example from the Gibeonites in Joshua 9. They came deceitfully and said that they were not from the Land of Israel, but they came from a foreign land, so their lives should be spared. The leaders of the Israelites swore. On the third day it was discovered that they had lied. It would have been just not to keep the oath, since it was given wrongfully, yet they kept it.[19] Further, the Gibeonites were the same people that the Torah had commanded, "*You shall not let a soul remain alive*" [Deuteronomy 20:16]. None of them should remain alive. They were godless people and idol-worshipers.

Testimony 3, Joshua 9.

---

17. Joshua 6:22–23.

18. A reference to Deuteronomy 7:1–5 and Deuteronomy 27, which appeared in Brenz's work. Both passages describe what the Israelites are to do when they enter the Land of Israel. Zalman's point was that they fulfilled all that God had instructed them to do.

19. Joshua 9:3–27.

Joshua 10.

In addition it is written, "*But the Israelites did not attack them, since the chieftains of the community had sworn to them*" [Joshua 9:18]. Israel did not kill them since the chieftains of Israel had sworn to them. How then should we, heaven forbid, swear falsely to the Christians?

2 Samuel 21. Saul allowed the Gibeonites to be killed, and there were three years of famine in the Land of Israel.

See 2 Samuel 21. There King Saul, of blessed memory, killed some of the Gibeonites. Thus there were three years of continuous famine in the Land of Israel. When the Holy One was asked, "What sin have we committed?" The Holy One said, "Because Saul had broken the oath and had killed the Gibeonites." So the Holy One was not satisfied until the Gibeonites were satisfied.[20]

They had to hang seven sons of Saul's household.

They had to hang seven royal children. This was against the rules of the Torah. First, "*Parents shall not die for their children, etc.*" [2 Chronicles 25:4]. The parents should not be killed because of the children, and the children because of the parents. Here the poor children had to die because of their father. It is written in the Torah, "*You must not let his corpse remain on the stake overnight, etc.*" [Deuteronomy 21:23]. These seven royal children had to hang the whole summer. Otherwise the Holy One would have punished the people and their children.[21]

The whole world must atone for false swearing, not just the one who has sworn falsely.

Here, the whole land had to suffer famine for three years, all so that we reflect on it and not swear uselessly or falsely by the name of the Holy One, whether against Gibeonites, Canaanites, or other people, good or evil. How should we swear falsely against Christians?

False swearing destroys land and people.

Our sages write and demonstrate from the verse that a false oath melts and destroys wood and stone more than fire and water.

Zalman Zvi took an oath in Wallerstein in *Heshvan* 5369.

I, Zalman Zvi, took an oath in Wallerstein, in *Heshvan* [October/November], 5369 [1609], because of aggravated circumstances. At the city hall, it was presented to me so sharply that it was not possible that Jews could be more threatened or the oath presented in a more difficult way.[22] Should I have had in mind to swear falsely, heaven forefend, I would have not sworn such a false oath for all the money in the world. I would also not take one hundred ducats to take such an oath again, even if I could do it truthfully. I was able to fulfill the above-mentioned oath with goodness

20. 2 Samuel 21:1–9.
21. 2 Samuel 21:10–14.
22. A reference to the "Oath More Judaico." See the Introduction.

and truth, thank God. There is no difference in the world with the oath, whether one does it against a Christian or a Jew. I call the apostate here a liar and a scoundrel.

10

Now the apostate writes again incorrectly. When a Jew wants to defraud another Jew, he says that the Christians have a false faith. That is, the Christians have false beliefs. Heaven forbid it. We do not say this for the reasons mentioned above. The Christians observe what has been presented to them. Everywhere when it is written "gentiles" [*goyim*], this does not mean Christians, but rather heathens and idol-worshipers.

11

Here the apostate again babbles at length about usury. He estimates what the gulden is worth this year and tells many more knavish things. Perhaps the apostate did them all himself. I have laid this out at length *in the book that I prepared for the Christians.* I have written much about how he took 5 percent interest every week on ten gulden from a Christian woman in Nordlingen whose name was Hegelisch. He also had good pledges. Thus he made 36 percent from the gulden this year (and not interest on interest). The hundred becomes one hundred and sixty-five, with interest. In contrast, we poor Jews take a little more than the Christians and often only the principal without interest is left. In contrast, we give large taxes and levies and have many hindrances, as are found in his majesty the emperor's freedoms that he has given us.

That usury is permitted us is not for our benefit.

I demonstrate in the book that I have written for the Christians that their majesties, the previous and present emperors, and those who gave us the freedoms to take interest, have rightfully and completely fulfilled the will of the Holy One. If you ask why, I will therefore tell you why. There is nothing better in the world than the farmer. A peasant sows the wheat and harvests thirty times what he sowed. He certainly has his bread, his cows, calves, butter, lard, flour, milk and meat, hens, geese, and everything he needs. However, we Jews have no land. Thus we must go to farms and landowners; to whoever has something to sell us. Concerning this, the sages of blessed memory said: The one who has to rely on the shopkeeper and baker is called someone who has not lived his life, thus we have been permitted usury as substitute. It causes us to be hated and despised, and is the cause of every misfortune that we must suffer from the Christians.

Zalman would prefer that Jews be permitted to engage in animal husbandry and agriculture, and that usury be forbidden.

If agriculture and animal husbandry were permitted to us, we would be able to leave the usury that causes us exile and all misfortunes. It is also about the usury and principal. One exists without money, and a peasant has it better and is more secure. One cannot carry away his field, and he cannot completely lose it, as often happens to us with usury. A piece of bacon bound to a pole.[23] Through this we are arrested and brought in. Concerning this Scripture said, "*The life you face shall be precarious*" [Deuteronomy 28:66]. Our life hangs from a thread, from nothing. We can buy bread, meat, milk, and what we need only if the peasants pay us when we lend to them. Usury is a curse and a punishment in the Torah. It causes us envy, as it is written, "*strife and anger.*" I do not need to elaborate. *It is enough with this for all who understand.*

12

The apostate now coos a whole bunch of mixed-up coos and wants to speak Hebrew. He says that we give the rulers bribes and says, "*the heavy heart that softens silver and gold.*" The words translate as, "He must have a hard heart, which gold and silver cannot soften." I cannot find this in his language.[24] The apostate, may his memory be blotted out, makes the accusation that the rulers take bribes. He writes in good German that we buy a duke and a manorial household, sparing no expense. However, you will find in Josephus, *The Romans*, the value of gold and silver. There is a dispute among three philosophers. One said that wine is the most valuable thing in the world. The second said a wife. The third said money.

13

The apostate writes that Jews do not consider adultery to be a sin if one can acquire money through it.

The apostate writes further that Jews do not consider adultery to be a sin if they can acquire money through it, and he cites a false story. He writes that it is written in [tractate] *Hullin*: There was a poor man who had a pretty wife, and a gentile lusted after her. He promised much money if he could have his way with her. The poor man sought advice from sages about how he should get the money from the gentile. The sages suggested that he should divorce his wife. Afterward she earned the money from the gentile and again remarried her husband. Woe to the apostate, the

23. This would appear to be a folk expression of some sort.

24. The second quote is what Brenz attempted to say, while the first is a literal translation of Brenz's confused Hebrew.

liar. Where is it written? What was it that so angered and upset Jacob's children that Shechem had violated their sister Dinah?

He had allowed himself to be circumcised, and he wanted to marry her. Yet afterward they destroyed and plundered all of Shechem.[25] How should a married woman have such a disgraceful permission?

Genesis 34.

Is it not written, "*No Israelite woman should be a prostitute*" [Deuteronomy 23:18]? No prostitute should be found among the daughters of Israel. "*Do not make your daughter a harlot*" [Leviticus 19:29]. You shall not give your daughter to harlotry or help it.

Deuteronomy 23.

The Ten Commandments, "*You shall not commit adultery*" [Exodus 20:13], and many more verses in the Torah, Prophets, and Writings, all forbid harlotry. What does the Holy One hate more than adultery? What happened with the incident of Zimri?[26] The apostate writes that they got divorced, and afterward she engaged in harlotry, and then they got remarried.

God hates harlotry.

It is written in Deuteronomy 24: "*If a man takes a wife, etc. and he writes her a bill of divorce, etc.*" [Deuteronomy 24:1]. "*She leaves his household and becomes the wife of another man, etc.*" [Deuteronomy 24:2]. "*Her first husband shall not take her to wife again*" [Deuteronomy 24:4]. This is when someone divorces his wife and she marries another man. If he dies or also gives her a divorce, then the first husband cannot remarry her. How should, heaven forbid, sages, of blessed memory, allow such a blasphemous and shameful thing? They do not permit more than what is written in the Torah. We are more careful about transgressions, thank God, more than all the other nations. All the books of the Christians themselves demonstrate this.

Deuteronomy 24.

14

Now the apostate writes things that are not in order and says that Jews spit on the back half [of the animal] that they sell to Christians, and wish them a poisonous death. This is the bitter death. I call on myself as a witness. In Rome, Venice, Prague, Cracow, Mantua, Hanau, and other places where there are many thousands of Jews who freely sell meat in butcher shops, dukes and nobles buy from them. Many in these places have had

The apostate writes that Jews spit on the meat they sell to Christians.

25. Genesis 34:21–29.
26. Numbers 25:6–15.

themselves baptized, but they cannot say this, since this is strictly forbidden to us, to curse or to spit on what is given to us by God as food. Our sages, of blessed memory, forbid this in many places. Whoever does this is fined.

15

The apostate writes that we give the gentiles meat from animals that have died as good meat for sale.

The apostate writes again: When a Jew's sheep dies, he gives it to the Christian. He says that he did not slaughter it properly, and it became religiously unfit [*trefah*]. He is not allowed to eat it. Until here his words. Above, the apostate always translates [the word] *trefah* as unclean. Now he says that we say it is *trefah*. If he would say that it was unclean, no Christian would buy it. He comes along very nicely and calls himself a liar, and says that *trefah* does not mean "unclean" but rather, as mentioned above, "broken and torn." However, the story happens to be a lie and a falsehood. All the sages forbid us from deceiving the Christians: the opposite of what the apostate said, that the Talmud permits us to deceive the gentiles all the time.

Hullin 94.

See [tractate] *Hullin* 94. "*It is forbidden to deceive a gentile, etc.*" It is forbidden to falsely convince and steal the heart of a gentile (one who worships idols). It cites a story: *Samuel crossed a body of water, etc.* Samuel crossed a body of water in the boat of a gentile. When he came to the other side, he ordered his servant to pay the boatman. The servant did this, and Samuel asked him how he had paid the boatman. Samuel became very angry with the servant, because the servant had given the boatman a *trefah* chicken instead of a properly slaughtered one. He also said that he had promised the boatman some good wine in partial payment, and he gave him wine mixed with water instead of good wine. That is why Samuel became angry, since one should not deceive anyone.[27]

Sanhedrin 94.

The Talmud writes further in [tractate] *Sanhedrin* 94b. One should not sell *trefah* meat to the gentiles, since one deceives them with this.

***Hoshen Mishpat*, section 228. It is forbidden to sell *trefah* meat as kosher meat to gentiles.**

See *Hoshen Mishpat*, section 228.[28] *It is forbidden to sell meat from an animal that died on the assumption that it had been slaughtered.* One should not

27. B. *Hullin* 94a.

28. Joseph Karo, *Shulchan Aruch* (first published Venice, 1565). *Hoshen Mishpat* is one of the four sections of the *Shulchan Aruch*, which is the standard code of Jewish law.

sell bad meat to the gentiles, as if it had been slaughtered. Our Talmud and all of our decisors forbid us to deceive any gentile (that is, one who worships idols) by selling them *trefah* meat as if it were kosher. How then would the Talmud allow us to deceive the Christians who believe in God? *His son the apostate answered falsely. I have expanded on this in the book that I have prepared for the Christians.*

16

The apostate writes that we do not consider murder to be a sin.

The apostate writes further that Jews do not consider murder and deadly assault to be sins. This does not need proof that it is a falsehood and a lie. The Ten Commandments say, "*Do not murder*" [Exodus 20:13]. There is written no difference among people, whether Christian, Turk, Tartar, or Jew. See in the *piyyut* for *Shavuot* what he writes about the prohibition against murder.[29]

Similarly, he writes that the Jews in Poland and Bohemia kill the informers and those who gossip against them. Also when someone wants to be baptized because of livelihood, they call this "permitted blood." *He answered falsely.* I have not heard this. Killing is forbidden. Yet there are fools who kill someone with their fists.

Chapter 1, paragraph 14.

Did not the apostate write above that the Jews identify those who gossip against them with an apple? They put it in the hand of the one they kill. However, this and this are both lies, bound together and united in the apostate's wickedness. Do we silence God and the ruler's household about what such an accused one had deserved?

17

The apostate writes one should ask the children what a church, a bell, and other things are called. That way we will find the truth, that we give their objects lowly and despicable names. The big old horse does not know anything. He does not understand Hebrew, German, or Italian, and he wants to learn much from the children. The apostate wrote his falsehoods. He did not think that Zalman Zvi of Aufhausen would uncover his scorn and contempt. It is not worth writing about or proving. Enough for the third chapter.

---

29. This is most likely a reference to the *Azharah* for *Shavuot*, a rhymed recitation of the 613 commandments.

CHAPTER 4

Herein the Jews respond with truth and purge that which the apostate of Oettingen, in his poisonous book, the *Schlangenbalg*, suspects us of, and clarify that they show complete sincerity in their relations with Christians. They pray for their majesties the rulers, and they do not mock or blaspheme. The Jewish physicians respond diligently to requests to heal Christians, and where it is God's will, to keep them alive. Therefore they are held in high regard and honored in all lands.

1

The apostate writes that Christians have no greater enemies than the Jews.

The apostate writes at the beginning of his fourth chapter that the Christians have no greater enemy on the earth than the Jews. Whatever practice the Christian has, the Jew does the opposite and says, "*This is the law of the gentiles.*" This is the Christian practice, etc. Regarding this, I say that I will demonstrate from all books that he is lying. See how the Egyptians tormented and confined us for hundreds of years.

Exodus 1.

Then the Holy One redeemed us and led us into the Land of Israel. The Holy One commanded us to treat the Egyptians, our enemies and tormentors, honestly and not to abuse them, as it is written,

Deuteronomy 23.

"*You shall not abhor an Egyptian, etc.*" [Deuteronomy 23:8]. You shall not consider an Egyptian unworthy, since you were a stranger in his land. At that time we had a government, king, and our own nobility, and would have been able to hold all of their offenses against them. Yet God forbade it.

No Egyptian, how much more so, no Christian to scorn.

How should we legally or rightly despise or scorn the Christians (who are not idolaters, as were the Egyptians)? Not only were we strangers in their land, but we are still an exiled and dispersed people who have no government or power. It is not only against God to despise the Christians, who do good for us, protecting and sheltering. It is also against nature and understanding. Should we do evil in return for good?

Proverbs 17.

Did not King Solomon say, "*Evil will never depart from the house of him who repays good with evil*" [Proverbs 17:13]? This means, one who returns evil for good. No evil leaves his house. When we do evil to the Christians who do good to us, then we have the curse in our houses. *Sefer Hasidim* writes that when a Christian asks a Jew for advice about which Jew he should do business with, which one is honest and which one dishonest, he should respond with the truth. He should warn the gentile if a Jew does not deal honestly.[1] It is also written in the above-mentioned book that if a Jew wants to beat a gentile unjustly, the Jew who sees this should help the Christian, and the Jew should remain there to help and support the one who is just.

One should also rise before old gentiles, lead them so they should not fall.

Our sages, of blessed memory, said, "*Rise before the aged*" [Leviticus 19:32], even before old gentiles who are heathens.[2] How much more so for Christians should one rise and honor them? One should lead and guide them so that they should not fall. The laws relating to gentiles forbid this, but this does not refer to Christians. Rather, it refers to the gentiles of the land of Canaan, who worshiped idols.

Leviticus 18.

As it is written, "*The practices of the land of Egypt . . . like the practices of the land of Canaan*" [Leviticus 18:3]. This is like the works of the land of Egypt and what the Canaanites did. You should not do what those whom I have expelled before you did. You should not follow in their ways. There are many such verses in the Torah and the Prophets. These do not speak about Christians. There were no Christians on the earth yet, regarding the matters called "laws of the gentiles."

***Shabbat*, page 67, what the laws of the gentiles and practices of the Amorites are.**

See in [tractate] *Shabbat*, where the practices of the Amorites are named. These are tricks and semi-magical idolatrous things.[3] We should not do them. The Christians also do not do these things. They also consider them wrong.

1. *Sefer Hasidism*, ed. Reuben Margulies (Jerusalem: Mosad Harav Kook, 1973), para.1086. I was not able to find the source of the second comment.
2. B. *Kiddushin* 32b.
3. B. *Shabbat* 67a–b.

The Torah also partially names them in Leviticus 19.[4] The Christians have many good statutes. If we do the opposite, we are dealing against the Torah. In conclusion, where it talks about laws of the gentiles, it means the idolaters, and not Christians. You have heard above why we call Christians "gentiles." However, in books we call Christians "Nazarenes" [*Nozrim*].

Leviticus 19.

2

The apostate writes further. When a Christian dies the Jew says, "An expiation [*kaparah*] has dropped dead." This is, he died like a dog. I say that the apostate is a liar and an ignoramus. He translates *peger* as a "dead dog." How do we say every day, "*who restores the souls of the dead* [*pegarim metim*]"?[5] Thus we must be praising God that He returns the souls to dead dogs and brings them back to life. The word *peger* refers to all corpses, whether Jew or Christian.

See Ezekiel 6. "*I will cast the corpses [pegarim] of the people of Israel*" [Ezekiel 6:5], "*the corpses [pegarim] of their kings*" [Ezekiel 43:7]. This means, I will give the corpses of the children of Israel, etc. with the corpses of their kings.[6]

Ezekiel 6; Ezekiel 43.

Amos 8. "*So many corpses left lying everywhere*" [Amos 8:3]. These are enough; there is no need to bring many examples. It is not an insult if one should say, "The Christian died [*pegert*]." However, that we should add expiation to it, meaning that his soul should be a sacrifice for our sins, as the apostate writes, is false. This is only when one of our enemies drops dead. So says a Jew about them. However, a Christian who has done nothing bad against us, we honor him and do not curse him. It is strongly forbidden.

Amos 8.

The apostate writes that we also say about them, "*His soul is in Gehenna.*" False. When he has done nothing to us Jews, we say, "*His soul should be at rest.*" His soul should be at rest. However, if someone has done harm to us, a Jew often says about him, "*His soul is in Gehenna.*" However, this is not often done or spoken. One does not say such words about an ordinary Christian.

Apostate writes that when a Christian dies we say, "*His soul is in Gehenna.*"

4. Leviticus 19:26–31.
5. The phrase is in the preliminary blessings of the morning prayers and is based on B. *Berakhot* 60b.
6. The same term, *peger*, is used for Jewish corpses and for the corpses of gentile kings, making them equivalent.

The apostate writes further that we say about dead Christians, "*The name of the evil gentile rots.*" I say that the disgraceful one wrongly translates his own insulting lies. There is no Christian and no extermination in these words.

Proverbs 10.

It is a verse from Proverbs that says, "*The name of the righteous is invoked for blessing, but the name of the wicked rots*" [Proverbs 10:7]. The memory of the pious should be remembered for good, but the name of the godless should rot. They should not be remembered. The verse talks about godless people and about Christians. There were no Christians then. We do not speak these words about any pious Christians. How then should the apostate prove his point? He proves it from the verse in Proverbs. We know that the pious Christians are not damned.

Three do not go to Gehenna.

The Talmud counts three who do not go to Gehenna or hell's fire. Among these three, one is a ruler who upholds justice, a government that upholds law and courts. The Christian emperor, dukes, and nobles do this.

Maimonides at the end of his book and the kabbalists write that the upright peoples have the world to come.

Rabbi Moses Maimonides writes at the end of his book that the upright peoples of the earth who are God-fearing, even if they do not keep the laws and Torah of Moses, still attain eternal life. Our sages, the divine philosophers, also write that the pious of the nations have a share in the world to come in the place where they write about the tree in the Garden of Eden.

If they fear the Lord.

How should we, contrary to our Talmud, our sages, and scribes, condemn the Christians who believe in God and uphold good justice and police protection?

The apostate writes about unspeakable curses that we wish on the Christians.

The apostate further writes many curse words and maledictions that we Jews supposedly say to Christians, heaven forbid, and many meaningless phrases and rumors about how we falsely receive thanks from Christians and wish them bad luck. When we give them food or drink, we wish that there should be poison in it. When we wish them a good *new year*, we say "a *bad year.*" In conclusion, he bundled together everything that he thought of. He cited it all, just like one counts out the dried twigs. Therefore, he made me much work to respond to all of his lies.

See what our sages write in many places. "*The law of the kingdom is the law.*"[7] This means, that which the king of the nation creates and commands is a strong law, and one is obligated to observe it; just like and even more so as if a king in Israel had commanded it. Therefore, it is forbidden to transgress the tax laws, since it is stealing. It belongs to the king.

The law of the kingdom is the law.

It is written in many places, "*It is forbidden to deceive a gentile.*" It is forbidden to deceive a gentile (even one who is an idol-worshiper). How much more so, one should not deceive any Christian. How does the apostate say that our Talmud permits doing all sorts of evil to Christians or gentiles? He says we curse and insult them secretly, with false words.

It is forbidden to deceive a gentile.

It is written in the Torah, "*Do not insult the deaf*" [Leviticus 19:14]. You should not curse a deaf person. That is, you should not curse the handicapped or speak with someone in an unfamiliar language that the other person does not understand. It is written that nobody should be excluded, whether they are Jew or gentile; cursing is forbidden. It is written near it, "*You shall fear your God, I am the Lord*" [Leviticus 19:14]. You shall fear your God, who knows everything you say. Therefore, you have two paths. If one follows the Torah and the words of the sages, he does not curse, maledict, or deceive anybody, whether a Jew or a Christian. However, if he does not follow the Torah, he does everything, then my writing will help much less. I only write to disprove the words of the apostate, that our Torah forbids all deceptions and falsehood. "*Everyone who deals dishonestly is abhorrent to the Lord your God*" [Deuteronomy 25:16]. It is an offense before God to deal unjustly. Therefore, one should not believe, heaven forbid, the lies of the apostates against the community of Israel.

Leviticus, 19. "*Do not insult the deaf.*"

King David talks about those with false hearts and who curse. "May the Lord cut off all flattering *lips*" [Psalms 12:4]. God should cut off all the divided false tongues.

Psalms 12.

One should receive both Christians and Jews with a faithful heart, as our sages, of blessed memory, said: "*Be first in greeting every person.*"[8] This means, be quick to greet and receive all people. There is no difference between a Christian and a Jew.

***Pirke Avot*: Be first in greeting every person.**

---

7. B. *Gittin* 10b and other places.

8. *Pirke Avot* 4.15.

Berakhot 17. It is written that one should greet all people, as the Talmud says in [tractate] *Berakhot* 17a, "*It was said about R. Yohanan ben Zakkai, etc.*" They said about R. Yohanan ben Zakkai that in his whole life no person was able to greet him first before he greeted them, including no gentile in the market. He always greeted Jews and gentiles in a friendly way. Why should we not greet the Christian?

Bottom of *Gittin* 62. At the bottom of [tractate] *Gittin* [62a], it is written explicitly that one should greet gentiles eagerly. I could bring proof many times, but it is enough with these.

5

The apostate writes further. The Jews call the Christian graves and tombs *unclean graves* [*kever tuma*]. This means "an unclean grave." So I say that the Cave of Machpelah and all the graves in which the dead lie are unclean. No *cohen* should walk on it. In ancient times, whoever touched the dead was unclean for seven days.

Numbers 19. Graves are impure, whether they are Jews' or gentiles'. "*And in the open, anyone who touches a person who was killed or who died naturally, or a human bone, or a grave, shall be unclean seven days*" [Numbers 19:16]. How then should I make a grave clean when the Torah makes it unclean? Now the apostate writes again about curses and says that we curse the Christians with "*he testifies falsely*" [Deuteronomy 19:18]. As mentioned above, cursing is forbidden. See what a lovely order the apostate has in his book. Now he writes about *impure graves* and then about cursing.

6

The apostate writes further in his book, *Schlangenbalg*. We call the Christians *orelim*.[9] This translates as "those who are stopped up," "those who do not know God." I say that this is not valid concerning us, that *orelim* should be translated as "the stopped-up ones," "those who do not know God."

Joshua 5. See what Joshua 5 writes. "*But He had raised up their sons in their stead; and it was these that Joshua circumcised, for they were uncircumcised*

9. The term *orel* (singular; *orelim*, plural) has several meanings, but with regard to people it means "one who is not circumcised." Thus it is sometimes a negative term for Christians, "the uncircumcised ones."

[*orelim*]" [Joshua 5:7]. This means, He put their children in their place. Joshua circumcised these children, because they were *orelim* [uncircumcised]. This means, with foreskins, and not yet circumcised, but not *orelim*, stopped-up ones, those who did not know God. They were pious people, and the Holy One performed miracles and wonders daily for them.

***Orelim* is not "stopped-up ones" who do not know God.**

Whenever *orelim* is written in the whole Torah it means "uncircumcised," those who still have their foreskins. So Martin Luther and other Christian commentators translate it.

Jeremiah 9.

However when Scripture speaks of evil people, it always writes "*uncircumcised of heart*," as the end of Jeremiah 9 writes, "*For all these nations are uncircumcised, but all the House of Israel are uncircumcised of heart*" [Jeremiah 9:25]. All nations are uncircumcised, still have their foreskins, but the House of Israel are uncircumcised of heart.

A Jew who is not circumcised is also an *orel*, Exodus 12.

A Jew who is not circumcised is also called an *orel*. "*No uncircumcised person [orel] may eat of it*" [Exodus 12:48]. No *orel* (that is, one who is uncircumcised) should eat the Paschal sacrifice. See what Ezekiel writes, "*Admitting aliens, uncircumcised of heart and uncircumcised of flesh, etc.*" [Ezekiel 44:7]. "*Thus said the Lord: Let no alien, uncircumcised of heart and uncircumcised of flesh, enter, etc.*" [Ezekiel 44:9]. Thus you find that there is a difference between uncircumcised of flesh and uncircumcised of heart. In conclusion, we call anyone who is not circumcised an *orel*. It is not a negative term, as the apostate ignoramus writes. He is uncircumcised of heart and uncircumcised of lips.

7

***Pesahim* 49. The youths who run around in the streets and do not study are called *sheketz*.**

The apostate writes further. We call the youths in the streets *sheigutz*. The fool wants to say *sheketz*.[10] This means "one who is worthless." I say that it is true that we call the youths on the streets this, including our children; all those who engage in villainy, running around in the streets, and not learning to read and write.

The Talmud, *Pesahim* 49, writes that nobody should marry an ignoramus, since the children that come from such a union are *sheketz*. This means,

10. *Sheketz* is the correct Hebrew pronunciation of the word. *Sheigutz* is the Yiddish pronunciation.

they are bunglers and unlearned people who are worthless and not careful.[11] This is why we call the youths in the streets (as the apostate himself writes) *sheketz*, because they do not want to study. However, we do not call anyone *sheketz* who holds himself as an honest person and desires to study. However, this does not mean that we would call a Christian a *sheketz*. This only happens with ignoramuses like the apostate who do not know the difference between studying and playing ball. Rather they think that anyone who is young should be called a *sheketz*. This term was first used in the Talmudic period when the heathens raised their children for no good purpose.

The Christians in this time are learned people and are not *sheketz*.

However, the Christians are different in this time and are not *sheketz*. Almost all of them study, and learning is esteemed among them.

Some do not respect learning very much.

Because of our many sins, it is the opposite among us. The Torah is worth little, and the whole world only shouts "money, money." Thank God, in Poland, Bohemia, and Italy, it is better than Ashkenaz. Yet one does find pious Ashkenazim, thank God, who do not turn away too much when one is learned; they still will intermarry with him. Therefore, because of our many sins, it is more beloved by our children than by us.

Though a pair of socks is as expensive in Ashkenaz as a jacket and coat in Poland.

Shekatzim are those who cannot study or learn; the rich who can study but do not want to. The poor will gladly study but cannot afford it, and so continue to travel.[12] *Sufficient for everyone who understands.*

8

Above, paragraph 4.

Now the apostate comes again and presents many curses and false words that we Jews supposedly give the Christians. This is all false and strongly forbidden. No honest Jew does this. It has been responded to above, in paragraph 4.

9

The apostate writes further. The Jews do not give alms to any Christian. They thank him with false words such as, "May Lot help you," and similar

11. B. *Pesahim* 49b.

12. A reference to the difficulties poor Jews had in finding a community that would give them permission to live there.

things. If they do give the Christian something, they do it for glory, that they should be praised for this. The Jew wishes him bad luck and poison in it. *Until here the words of the apostate.* I say that our holy books are full [of statements] that we are obligated to give charity to gentiles, just as we are obligated to give charity to Jews.

See what is written in [tractate] *Baba Bathra.* Each person is obligated to feed and nourish the nations of the world (these are people who worshiped idols), just like Jews.[13]

Baba Bathra, page 9.

Yore Deah, section 251.[14] "*Whoever extends his hand, etc.*" You should give charity to all those who raise their hands and desire charity, including a gentile.

Yore Deah, section 251.

Hullin, page 61,[15] writes, and also Maimonides, in *Laws of Charity*,[16] that one is obligated to give charity to gentiles.

Hullin, page 61; Maimonides, _Laws of Charity._

Sefer Zedah la-Derekh writes:[17] "*We feed the poor of the nations of the world, we visit their sick, we bury their dead and eulogize them, we comfort their mourners, and we do not deny their poor the poor's share of the crops.*"[18] This is translated: We should feed the poor of the nations, we visit the sick, we bury their dead, mourn them, and we console the mourners. We should also not deny them picking what was forgotten in the field and the vineyard; thus in every way as if they were Jews. I could cite much more. I have cited much more *in the book that I wrote for the Christians.* However, why should we write much about the charity that we should give to gentiles? Sadly, the Jews are not given much charity, even by their friends. *Deliver us, O God, our deliverer, have mercy on the poor who are insulted. May they be justified in Your eyes. Give a heart of flesh to the rich and remove the heart of stone.*[19]

Zedah la-Derekh, ma'amar 2, chapter 3.

---

13. It is implicit in B. *Baba Bathra* 9a.
14. *Shulchan Aruch*, *Yore De'ah* 251.2, in the commentary *Siftei Cohen.*
15. This should be B. *Gittin* 61a.
16. Maimonides, *Mishneh Torah*, *Laws of Charity*, 7.7.
17. Menahem ben Zerach, *Zedah la-Derekh* (Ferrara, 1554; 2d ed., Sabbioneta, 1567).
18. The three types of leavings after the harvest that are left for the poor are called *leket*, *shikhah*, and *peah* in Hebrew.
19. Some of these phrases are taken from Ezekiel 11:19, but they are not direct quotations.

10

The apostate says that no Jew goes out of the house of a Christian without having stolen.

The *Schlangenbalg* writes further that no Jew goes out of a Christian's house without having stolen. He takes either a small wooden or straw handle, and with this he takes away the Christian's luck. I say, what kind of thief steals this? No Jew does this thing with the straw or wood, even if he is a thief. It is magic or ways of the Amorites, and is forbidden. It is foolishness to say that one takes away the Christian's luck. Perhaps he also takes away the bad luck.

11

The apostate writes that the Talmud teaches us to take away the Christian's luck.

The apostate writes further in the following words: "The Talmud allows and teaches how a Jew should take away the luck of a rich Christian. He should take earth from the four corners of the Christian's house and bury it under his threshold." The apostate lies about the Talmud like a scoundrel. Let him show me where this is found? As mentioned above, the response is that this is magic or the ways of the Amorites.

12

The apostate writes that no gentile is acceptable to us as a witness.

The apostate writes further: "No Christian was taken and accepted by the Jews as a witness." He cites an amusing expression in Hebrew here that is laughable. I say that it is written in one place that gentiles are not believed with regard to certain matters. However, those whom the Talmud writes about are idolatrous heathens, as has often been demonstrated. However, Christians are certainly accepted as witnesses.

Psalm 144.

David wrote that we did not accept testimony from the idolatrous nations "*whose mouths speak lies, etc.*" [Psalms 144:8], since their mouths are full of falsehood, and to show them good is a false goodness. King David writes this about the heathens and not about the Christians. There were no Christians yet. However, we believe the oath of a Christian, since they believe that swearing falsely is a big sin. Where we should not believe the Christian are in those things that touch on our religion, and the Christian does not believe in them, and does not consider them a sin.

Concerning what does one not believe a Christian?

When a Christian says: "Jew, eat this meat, it is kosher; a Jew has slaughtered it or inspected it," here I do not need to believe him, since he is making me stumble. He does not consider it a sin if he gives me pork instead of beef. Concerning this, our scholars say,

"Do you want to believe that the gentile makes pork kosher for you?" However, regarding that which a Christian considers to be a sin, or swears an oath on, you may certainly believe him.

Should one believe a gentile who says pork is kosher?

See in the *Responsa* of Rabbi Jacob Weil. He writes that the Christians are to be trusted, and their words are to be believed. *It occurred to me in the year 5368* [1608] in the month of *Ab*. The wife of a butcher from the village of Ratingen put false signs on nonkosher meat and sold it to Jews in Aufhausen. She said: "I had it slaughtered and inspected. I accidentally came upon this." I beat her and took the meat away. I brought her to the ruler and accused her. She said before the ruler that it doesn't hurt that we behaved in this way. They didn't die from it. Therefore, we should not believe them regarding such things on their word alone, since they gladly cause us to stumble.

Responsa **of Rabbi Jacob Weil, section 147.**

13

The apostate further writes a new lie about the Talmud. He says it is written in [tractates] *Shabbat* and *Erubin*, "*The nations of the world are not called men but cattle.*" He translates this, "Christians should not be considered people, since they live without faith, like livestock." *May God cut off my lips in pieces*, where is this written? It does not mean "cattle." The nations of the world who are idol-worshipers are called not human.

As David said, "*Man does not abide in honor; he is like the beasts that perish*" [Psalms 49:13]. A person who does not want to pay attention to God's majesty and honor is compared to livestock. David did not say this about Christians (there were no Christians yet on the earth), but rather he spoke about the heretics and idolatrous nations. Christians believe in God. They observe the Ten Commandments and everything that is imposed on them.

Psalms 49.

See in *Sanhedrin*. Rabbi Meir said: "Where you find a gentile who studies Torah and observes the seven commandments of the children of Noah, he is as good as a high priest."[20]

Sanhedrin, page 59. "*A gentile who studies Torah is like the high priest.*"

We learn from the verse, "*By the pursuit of which man shall live*" [Leviticus 18:5]. The person who fulfills the commandments will have life from it. It is written "a person" and not a priest, Levite, or Israelite. This shows that

Leviticus 18.

20. B. *Sanhedrin* 59a.

each person on the earth, whoever observes the seven commandments of the children of Noah, has eternal life. The Christians observe even more. Why should we not consider them people? They were not commanded to keep the Torah. Thus you see that the Talmud calls all nations, even the idolatrous nations, "man" or "people." However, since Christians attach the Trinity to the unity [of God], therefore they are not mentioned by name, since it is not forbidden in the seven commandments of the children of Noah. *See in Sefer Mitzvot Katan.*[21]

14

The apostate writes further. The Jews say that the Christians have no marital obligations. When a Jew sleeps with a gentile woman, he has not broken his marriage. We allow it because she is unclean. *These are the words of the apostate.* I have demonstrated above that the idol-worshiping heathens did not make their wives common, they strongly upheld marriage, and their children are not bastards.

Sanhedrin, page 58.

See in *Sanhedrin.*[22] Our sages say that the verse says, "*Hence a man leaves his father and mother and clings to his wife*" [Genesis 2:24]. Therefore, a man should leave his father and mother and cleave to his wife. He should cleave to his wife, but to no other wife. From this we learn that the children of Noah had marital obligations. How much more so, the Christians have marital obligations. However, that we (as the apostate writes) violate nothing when someone sleeps with a Christian woman, these are his lies. Zimri, son of Salu, had illicit sex with Cozbi, daughter of Zur. Phinehas stabbed him, and the Lord God was completely satisfied.[23] How is it not a sin to break the marriage vows with a Christian? This was only a heathen, and yet he was punishable by the death penalty.

Sanhedrin, page 81, one who sleeps with a gentile woman can be pursued, etc.

See [tractate] *Sanhedrin*, page 81.[24] One who breaks his marriage vows with a gentile woman, the next one who sees him should stab him to death. If he is not killed by people, then the Holy One will cause him to die before his allotted time. It is true, what he writes, that we consider the

---

21. By Isaac of Corbeil (d. 1280), containing abbreviated discussions of the commandments. First published in Constantinople (1510) and reprinted many times thereafter.
22. B. *Sanhedrin* 58a.
23. Numbers 25:6–11.
24. B. *Sanhedrin* 81a.

Christian women to be unclean. We consider our wives, who have the Torah, also unclean when they do not go to the ritual bath to purify themselves from their menstrual bleeding.

15

The apostate writes further that we make a distinction when we mention a Jew and a Christian. We call them unclean and the children of Satan. This is false. The Christians are not of the devil. The devil cannot create people; only God the Lord. *Thus, we all have one father, and one God created us.*

16

The apostate again writes a falsehood about the Talmud and says that, when we Jews pass through a place where the majority are Christians, we must curse all the grain and fruit or vegetation of that place. Heaven forbid, let the apostate show this, where we curse God's vegetation.

The apostate writes that we curse the gentile's grain and fruits.

Is it not written, "*when you besiege a city*" [Deuteronomy 20:19]? When a city was besieged, we were not supposed to chop down any fruit-bearing trees. These were enemies. How should we, heaven forbid, curse the fruit of the Christians? The lie is against nature. We Jews have no agriculture. We must buy food from the Christians. What greater misfortune can there be, heaven forbid, as when it is expensive?

Deuteronomy, end of chapter 20.

Did not David say, "*You put joy into my heart when their grain and wine show increase*" [Psalms 8:4]? You give joy into my heart when their grain and wine increase. Thus today we pray five times every day, including the cantor's repetition of the *Amidah*, and we say, "*Bless for us, etc.*," that we call upon God, that all sorts of grain should be plentiful.

Psalms 4, Shprinza, the wife of Zalman Zvi, experienced this.

On Passover we pray for *tal* [dew], asking God to provide blessed dew.

Passover, *Tal*.

On *Sukkot* we pray for rain, that God should give us blessed rain. You find in [tractate] *Berakhot* the opposite of what the apostate writes. We are obligated to recite a blessing when we see beautiful fruit in the field.[25] *I have expanded in the book that I have prepared for Christians.*

***Sukkot*, we pray for rain.**

25. B. *Berakhot* 43b.

17

The *Schlangenbalg* writes: When a Christian sees many Jews and he wonders and says, "How many Jews is this?" the Jew says, "Eye to an expiation, too many Jews for your eyes."[26] This means the Christian's eyes should jump out of his head. See how he makes himself a liar in his own words? "Too many for your eyes" does not translate as "to jump out." Jews do not like it when someone wants to count them. The [Israelites] were warned.

Seventy thousand Israelites died, 2 Samuel 24.

King David counted Israel, and seventy thousand died.[27] The Holy One said, "*When you take a census of the Israelite people, etc. . . . that no plague may come upon them*" [Exodus 30:12]. When they counted the Israelites, they had to give half a shekel, so that no plague should come among them. King Saul took a lamb from each one and afterward counted the lambs.[28] In conclusion, nobody is happy when somebody shouts at them. When somebody says about a child, "What a nice, big, or fat child this is," the mother says, "Your evil eye should not harm my child." So we also say, "Your eyes too many." This means, you have large, far-seeing eyes. You think that we have too much. However, these words do not have the meaning of a curse or eyes jumping out.

18

The apostate writes that the Talmud says it would be good if no Jew spoke with a gentile on the Sabbath, so that he does not desecrate the Sabbath by eventually engaging in business. I admit this; it would be very good.

Isaiah 58.

You find in Isaiah 58. "*If you refrain from trampling the Sabbath, from pursuing your affairs on My holy day etc. . . . and if you honor it and go not your ways and look to your affairs, nor strike bargains*" [Isaiah 58:13]. Thus you find that speaking on the Sabbath is forbidden. However, the apostate writes that the Talmud permits debts to be demanded and collected on the Sabbath. This is a lie and a falsehood. No Jew does this.

Roland 17, 18, testifies that Jews do not sue anyone on the Sabbath; therefore, one should not attempt to sue them on the Sabbath.

See what the highly learned man, Rolando, proves.[29] The Jews do not sue on the Sabbath. Therefore, one should also not sue them on the Sabbath. This does not have to be proven, as it is contemporary, and all the Christians know it well.

---

26. This is garbled and not a recognizable expression.
27. 2 Samuel 24:15.
28. B. *Yoma* 22b.

19

The apostate writes further that the Jews gather on the Sabbath and boast about how they deceived the Christians during the whole week. In addition, they say to the listeners that everything should be done to the Christians. They should tear their hearts out from their bodies, and they say the best of the gentiles should be killed. This means one should kill the best of the Christians. Also, when they hear that a Jew deceived a Christian, they say to each other the Jews have brought a sacrifice. Until here the words of the apostate. Concerning this, I say that the apostate may have heard this in a gathering of idlers who were boasting about how they deceived people. However, no upright Jew boasts or speaks in this manner, whether on the Sabbath or during the week, much less that one should tear out the heart from a Christian's body. We should not deceive anyone, whether Christian or Jew, as mentioned above.

20

However, that which is written, "The best of the gentiles should be killed," does not refer to Christians; rather, it concerns the gentile idol-worshipers. The Jerusalem Talmud writes that this relates to a war. The Talmud says that when one wages war with the gentiles (that is, with the heathens), one should not allow any of them to escape, and you should not spare anyone. You should kill even the best of them (that is, the most important or the king). If you let him escape, he will see your weaknesses, and he might recover and eventually destroy you.[31]

The best of the gentiles should be killed.[30]

It cites an example. King Saul had compassion for King Agag and did not want to kill him.[32] As a result, Haman arose and wanted to destroy all of them.[33] Ahab, the king of Israel, let the king of Aram live and called him brother. Thus the prophet said to the king:

1 Samuel 15.

"*Because you have set free the man whom I have doomed, your life shall be forfeit for his life and your people for his people*" [1 Kings 20:42]. The Holy One said

1 Kings 20.

29. It is not clear to whom this is a reference (Roland/Rolando are references to the same person). From the context, he might be the author of a law code of some sort.
30. *Mekhilta de-Rabbi Yishmael, Beshallah*, 1.
31. J. *Kiddushin* 4.9.
32. 1 Samuel 15:9.
33. B. *Megillah* 13a.

to the king, "Because you have released the condemned man, your body, your city, and your people will stand instead of his people." Concerning this, the Talmud says, "*The best of the gentiles should be killed. Even with the best of the snakes, crush its head.*"[34] The best among the heathens (when you wage war against them), kill them, since when he sees his chance and becomes strong again, he will destroy you. The best of the snakes, crush its brains, since when you let it sleep, it will seek to kill you. Therefore you strike first, as the example with the snake and the peasant shows. However, when it is not war, we do not kill any heathen who worships idols. How much more so a Christian who believes in God? I have written at length about this above. This apostate wants to explain this text to our detriment.

21

When a ruler does good for the Jews, he follows his messiah.

The apostate writes more. When a ruler does something good for us, we say that the ruler has no faith in Yeshua the Nazarene. Tell him that the apostate is lying, and I say the opposite. When a ruler does good for the Jews, he is obeying their messiah, as mentioned above. He had prayed for us himself, and does not want for us to be repudiated. All the most important leaders of Christendom and the pope himself (he is certainly a good Christian) defend and protect the Jews, thank God. The apostate knows as much about his own faith as he had previously known about Judaism.

22

The apostate writes that the physicians give poison to the Christians.

The apostate writes and warns all Christians about the Jewish physicians. He says that we consider it a positive commandment to kill many Christians, like a *mohel* who circumcises many children. This has often been responded to above, that we are not supposed to kill any gentile, even one who is an idol-worshiper. Is it not written, "*Whoever sheds the blood of a man, by man shall his blood be shed*" [Genesis 9:6]? The one who spills a person's blood, his blood should also be spilled. At that time there was no Jew and no Christian on the earth. No person should be killed. Is it also not written, "*You shall not murder*" [Exodus 20:13]?

Pirke Avot 2.

Is it not written in *Pirke Avot* that Hillel saw a skull floating on the water? He said, "*Because you drowned, etc.*" Because you drowned someone, so you were also drowned, and in the end the one who drowned you will also be drowned.[35] It was certainly not written on the skull whether it was a Jew

34. J. *Kiddushin* 4.9.

or a Turk. It is only justice from God. The one who kills a person will also be killed. How should we venture to be so evil to kill a Christian who trusted us and asked for help from our physicians?

However, where our physicians are found, they are highly praised and held in high esteem, thank God, in the most important places, like Rome, Venice, Prague, Paris, Constantinople, and other places. No baptized Jew has ever poured out such lies in the circumstances. God and the authorities will not allow such a lying mouth and insulter of honor to go unpunished.

Jewish physicians are held in high esteem in all places.

23

The obtuse apostate writes: Jews have a tradition that when a *mohel* circumcises as many [male infants] as are equivalent to the numerical value of his name, then he enters the Garden of Eden. O the fool! If a *mohel* is called David, he quickly enters the Garden of Eden. However, if his name is Methuselah, then he will certainly remain outside. My name is Solomon, and I am a *mohel*, thank God. Thus (according to the apostate's words), I must have three hundred and seventy-five to enter.[36] We only believe that whoever fulfills many commandments has much reward, whether his name is David or Solomon.

24

Now the apostate writes that Jews say that the Holy One rests on the hands of the priests [*kohanim*] when they bless the people, and whoever sees this goes blind. The apostate brazenly looked at it and did not become blind. In the book I wrote for the Christians, I demonstrated that the reason is because of madness. We frighten the children with this so that they should not shout or make obscene gestures to the priests, as *The Mordechai* writes.[37]

It is written nowhere that one becomes blind, but rather he gets dark eyes,[38] and specifically when the Temple existed. However, the apostate

***Mordechai* writes the reason why one should not look at the hands of the priests.**

35. M. *Avot* 2.7.
36. In Hebrew the numerical value of "David" is 14, "Methuselah" is 784, and "Solomon" is 375.
37. This is an important medieval halakhic work by Rabbi Mordechai ben Hillel (d. 1298).
38. Another way of saying that his eyesight deteriorates.

must have been an insolent, big fool that he brazenly looked at this, and did not at least cover one eye. It would be just if he became blind in both eyes at the same time. However, in truth he was already blind and is still blind. Therefore he dared to do it.

25

The apostate further mocks the story of the destruction of the Temple and Kamza and Bar Kamza. The apostate says that, as a result, we have no other reason for the destruction of the Temple. It is all because Bar Kamza was embarrassed. *I have written at length in my book for the Christians.* We say that unfortunately we committed other sins, and because of this story, Titus and Vespasian came to the Land [of Israel] and destroyed the Temple.[39]

Josephus writes how it happened.

We learn from this that nobody should embarrass his friend. However, this was not the main sin. Unfortunately, we sinned too much with other sins.

26

The apostate further throws the Karaites before us. He says that we have no faith. We have two types of customs in the Rhineland and similarly with our prayers. The foolish apostate has not read his Gospels.

Matthew, Mark, Luke.

It is often written there about Sadducees and Pharisees. Josephus also often talks about the Pharisees, Sadducees, and Essenes. What do we care about the Sadducees or Karaites? They are not worth following, since they believe in the literal interpretation of Scripture and not in the Oral Torah. It is written, "*No Ammonite or Moabite shall be admitted into the congregation of the Lord*" [Deuteronomy 23:4]. From this our sages, of blessed memory, learn, an Ammonite man and not an Ammonite woman, a Moabite man and not a Moabite woman. The men of Ammon and Moab should not enter Israel, but the women may.[40] The Sadducees contradict themselves about this. According to their words, King David, who was descended from Ruth, the Moabite, would be unfit. So too, Yeshua the Nazarene would also be an unfit descendant, since the Christians make him a descendant of David.

---

39. B. *Gittin* 55b–56a.
40. B. *Yevamot* 77b.

Thus Jews and Christians must recognize that the sages, of blessed memory, are right in this instance, and the Sadducees and Karaites were wrong. The sages have the tradition from Sinai. However, the differences in customs and prayers are not different with regard to the principles of the faith. It depends on the land and its sages. *It is not to be discussed at length [here]. I have discussed it at length in my book for the Christians.*

Christians must recognize that the Karaites were wrong and the sages, of blessed memory, were right.

The apostate writes further[41] that we think that we earn the world to come with gluttony and excessive drinking, since we say that whoever eats three meals on the Sabbath has earned the world to come. We also say that each Jew has two souls, with which you can engage in more gluttony. Until here, the words of the apostate. I say that in truth it is a great positive commandment to honor the Sabbath.

Isaiah 58, *"If you call the Sabbath delight."*

Isaiah 58, "*If you call the Sabbath delight etc.*" [Isaiah 58:13]. However, for what relates to the additional soul, turn to the kabbalistic sages. However, the apostate had no soul at all, even on the Sabbath. We do not need a soul to eat, but a stomach. The soul is spiritual and not physical. The additional soul exemplifies that we should study and pray. The soul derives benefit from this. The spices that we smell on Saturday night allude to this. It is like when a good friend comes to the house, and when it gets dark, they depart. We also say it in the priestly blessing, "Give light and praise, spices and wine for the way."[42] *May God pour out peace on us, and may He make us worthy of the day that is completely Sabbath and the rest of eternal life.*

41. In the "List of the Apostate's Accusations" at the end of the text, Zalman Zvi includes a paragraph 27, which suggests that the numeral 27 should appear at the beginning of this paragraph. However, the number is not found in any of the editions. This must have been an error on the part of the printer, who forgot to add the paragraph number.
42. An allusion to the *Havdalah* ceremony, which concludes the Sabbath.

CHAPTER 5

Herein we Jews demonstrate that we pray for the peace of the Christian king and emperor and the ordinary people. The apostate from Oettingen lied about us in his poisonous book, the *Schlangenbalg.*

1

The apostate writes that we curse their messiah and all those who believe in him.

The apostate writes at the beginning of his fifth chapter of his book, the *Schlangenbalg*: The Jews curse Christ and all those who believe in him. I have often shown that we are not supposed to curse anyone on the earth. See [tractate] *Berakhot*, page 7, which cites a story. There was a godless man, a heretic who caused great troubles for a sage. The sage wanted to determine the exact moment when the Holy One gets angry. (This is one second every day, and when someone curses during that moment, it is fulfilled.) He wanted to curse that heretic and evildoer. Before the appointed time, the sage fell asleep, and when he awoke, the time had already passed. The sage said: "Now I see that the Holy One did not want even one evildoer to be cursed."[1] Why should we curse the Christians who believe in the Holy One?

2

The apostate says that the Jews pray for great curses.

The apostate writes further. We say in our prayers, "*Zamdu be-kabzekha shashua la-tola.*" This means, "Bind the Christians with Your wrath, all those who hope for Christ." *Until here his words.* I do not find this in any book. According to his own words, *Zamdu* means "remove him." *Be-kabze-kha* means "your ingathering." *Shashua* has no meaning. *La-tola* to *tola.*[2]

1. B. *Berakhot* 7a.
2. This word, *tola,* can mean "worm" or "hanged one."

3

Another curse.

The apostate writes further. We pray, "*Ten kevodekha la-tola.*" This means, "Why do you want to give your honor to the hanged one?" This is Christ. I will translate each of his words. *Ten* means "give." *Kevodekha*, "your honor." *La-tola*, "to the worm." I have not seen this word in any book in all my days.

4

The apostate says that the Jews spit on Yeshua the Nazarene and on all Christians.

Now he comes to *Alenu le-Shabeah.* He says that we say: "*They bow down to, etc.*" This means, the Christians bow down to foolishness and emptiness, and pray to a god who cannot help them. Afterward, we spit three times, against Christ and all those who believe in him. Also, the word *va-req* has the same numerical value as *Yeshu* [Jesus].[3] This is how we curse and spit in secret. Concerning this, I say that it is a public falsehood.

Joshua established *Alenu* against the Canaanites.

One. Joshua composed *Alenu* against the nations in Canaan who worshiped idols and bowed to nonsense and emptiness many thousands of years before Christ's birth.[4] Second, it must be that the numerical value can have no evil intention or meaning against Yeshua the Nazarene, since it is written shortly afterward [in the *Alenu* prayer], "*His glorious abode is in the highest heaven.*" "*His glorious*" [*yeqaro*] also has the numerical value of *Yeshu* [Jesus]. According to this we confess that Jesus sits in the highest heaven. Whoever says this is no Jew, but a Christian. The apostate took this number from the evil book of the apostate Anthonius Margaritha,[5] who cites *va-req*, as mentioned above.

The apostate brings a false number.

The apostate did not understand the matter and added the word *le-hevel* [to nonsense] and gets the number wrong. *About him I say, and he also brought nonsense.* We do not deal with such nonsense, since Christians bow to God, creator of heaven and earth. However, they make Yeshua the Nazarene a trinity, but they do not deny the unity [of God] with this, as I have mentioned above. *I have expanded on this in the book that I wrote for the Christians.*

3. The numerical equivalence in Hebrew is accurate.

4. This tradition is found in a number of medieval works. See E. E. Urbach, ed., *Arugat ha-Bosem*, vol. 3 (Jerusalem: Mekizei Nirdamim, 1963), 468–71.

5. On Margaritha and his anti-Jewish writings, see the Introduction.

5

Now the apostate writes: We pray in the Grace after Meals, "*May the Merciful One break the yoke of the nations from our neck; may He lead us in dignity to our land.*" This is translated: God should break the yoke of Christian rule that has been given over us. Look at the falsehoods of the apostate. No Christian is mentioned; it means merciful God. Break the yoke that the nations burdened us with, and lead us publicly into our land. Where is it written that the Christian government should be broken?

The apostate writes that we pray to God to destroy the Christian rule.

I believe that the Christians would gladly see us come into our land. They would bid us farewell and accompany us to the ship on which we will travel there. The Turks have something to say, because we want to take our land back, which they control at the present. The Christians would certainly answer amen to this, "*May the Merciful One*" [*Ha-Rahaman*].[6]

Christians would be glad to see us move to our own land.

This prayer comes from the verse: "*I broke the bars of your yoke and made you walk erect*" [Leviticus 26:13].

Leviticus 26.

6

Now the apostate comes and writes that we pray: "*The kingdom of wickedness should speedily be uprooted.*" This is translated as: "The wanton Christian kingdom should be destroyed." One may laugh at how he writes. He writes: "*The kingdom of wickedness should be speedily deya'agar.*"[7] It was responded to above. The kingdom of wickedness is not Christian. However, I will respond at greater length when I come to "*and the apostates.*"

The apostate translates "kingdom of wickedness" as the Christians.

Now he comes to "*Our Father, Our King, destroy the evil decree of our judgment.*" This is translated as "destroy all the Christians." This needs no testimony that the ignoramus apostate is lying. It applies to us and means that we pray to God that he should break the evil decree. Since the Holy One decreed it, he should break it. It has no mention of Christians or any other nation.

An unrhymed falsehood.

---

6. This is the opening phrase of a series of invocations found in the Grace after Meals (*Birkat ha-Mazon*).
7. The last word is a nonsense word and an example of Brenz's ignorance.

Psalms 139. The Holy One writes all the deeds of people. In Psalm 139 the verse says, "*They were recorded in Your book*" [Psalms 139:16]. They were all recorded in Your book.

Jeremiah 22. Jeremiah, "*Record the man as without succession*" [Jeremiah 22:30]. Inscribe these separately.

Isaiah 65. Isaiah, "*See, this is recorded before Me, etc.*" [Isaiah 65:6]. It was written before Me.

Jeremiah 15.[8] "*Do not let their sins be blotted out before You*" [Nehemiah 3:37]. You should not erase their sins before Your eyes.

Psalms 58. *With Your great mercy, blot out my sins.*[9] With Your great compassion, leave out my misdeeds.

Psalms 29. *Remember the sin of his fathers, etc.*[10] "*All who are inscribed for life in Jerusalem, etc.*" [Isaiah 4:3]. Thus everything is written before the Holy One. Therefore we pray to the Holy One that He should tear up the note on which our sins are written.

8

The apostate says that we pray on *Rosh Hashanah* that God should send great wars and other great curses on Christendom. The apostate further says that we pray on *Rosh Hashanah* that *God should wage war on the Cutheans and their rulers*. This means God will send war on dukes and rulers, and all of Christendom. A cloud should cover them with scabs and leprosy. He should kill them and destroy them with His wrath, and wound the rulers of the earth. I say that this does not refer to Christians but to Cutheans. They were a godless, idolatrous people who did great harm to us in ancient times.

2 Kings 17; who are the Cutheans? See who they are in 2 Kings 17. The king of Assyria settled them in Samaria. They were idol-worshipers and were called Cutheans because they came from the land of Cuth.[11] It is now called Calicut.

8. This reference is incorrect. It should be Nehemiah 3.
9. This is not a biblical verse. The reference to Psalms 58 is not clear. The verse closest to this is Psalms 51:3.
10. This is also not a biblical verse. Similarly, the reference to Psalms 29 is not clear.
11. 2 Kings 17:24–41.

These Cutheans caused us great troubles when Ezra and the Israelites left Babylon and went to the Land of Israel. See in Ezra-Nehemiah that Nehemiah prayed, "*Do not cover up their iniquity, etc.*" [Nehemiah 3:37].

Ezra 4, Nehemiah 3 and 6.

Yalkut writes how Ezra and his court excommunicated the Cutheans with three hundred priests, three hundred Torah scrolls, and three hundred shofars.[12] Therefore, as an eternal memorial, we still curse them, *for they are excommunicated.* However, heaven forbid, we should curse the Christians.

Ezra, *Yalkut*, page 36; Ezra excommunicated the Cutheans.

9

The apostate further disgraces three words. He says that we say, "*Arise and carry my transgressions,*" and he writes harsh curses that we give the Christians, heaven forbid. This prayer is neither against Christians nor against any nation in the world. On the contrary, we pray to the Holy One that He should allow the day to come soon so that all the nations will become one and worship one God. The following is the meaning of the prayer. "*Arise . . . assert yourself against the fury of the foes*" [Psalms 7:7]. "*Kerev yom yelchu nozrim. Reyim lehiyot ve-taburim. Reutam derichat bozrim.*" These are all verses from the Prophets and Writings.

The apostate writes great curses that we give to the Christians, heaven forbid.

"*Arise . . . assert yourself against the fury of the foes*" [Psalms 7:7]. "*Kerev yom yelchu nozrim. Reyim lehiyot ve-taburim. Reutam derichat bozrim,*" etc.[13] All this relates to the Day of Judgment. We are not cursing anyone. *I have expanded on this in the book that I prepared for the Christians,* and I will prove that this will only happen in the days of Gog and Magog.

Psalms 7, Jeremiah 51.

10

The apostate writes that we pray, "*And He will overturn the thrones of the kingdoms on the earth.*" God should overturn the thrones of the kingdoms of the earth. This also is no curse, as mentioned above. The majority of the prayers of *Rosh Hashanah* and *Yom Kippur* refer to this, that we pray that the Holy One should soon bring the day when all the nations and kingdoms will recognize Him as Lord.

---

12. *Yalkut Shimoni*, 2 Kings, *Remez* 234.

13. These words are not found in the Bible, and their meaning is unclear.

End of Zephaniah. The end of Zephaniah says, "*But wait for Me, says the Lord, etc.*" [Zephaniah 3:8]. "*For then I will make the peoples pure of speech, so that they all invoke the Lord by name, and serve Him with one accord*" [Zephaniah 3:9]. This means, therefore, "Hope for Me," says God. "At the same time, I want to give all the nations a pure speech, so that all of them will call on the name of God and worship Him in holiness."

End of Joel. The end of Joel, "*I will gather all the nations and bring them down to the Valley of Jehoshaphat, etc.*" [Joel 4:2].

Zechariah 14. "*And the Lord shall be king over all the earth*" [Zechariah 14:9]. God will be king over the whole earth. Thus, the prayer was based on God. The apostate took pieces of it, so that it sounds this way. "*His kingship over the whole earth*" [Zechariah 14:9]. "*Shout aloud, O depths of the earth*" [Isaiah 44:23]. "*Let the heavens rejoice and the earth exult*" [Psalms 96:11]. "*And He will overturn the thrones of kingdoms*" [Haggai 2:22]. "*All who have breath in their nostrils in the land will say, 'How majestic is Your name throughout the earth'*" [Psalms 8:2]. "*He will awaken those who sleep in the earth.*" This explicitly talks about the Day of Judgment and the resurrection of the dead, and not that we are cursing a people.

11

Similar to this the apostate says, "*Every height will fall, mountains and valleys will be brought low, all the nation shall be covered by fog.*" The apostate translates this as: "All the heights, mountains, and valleys, he will cause to fall over the whole nation of Christendom." *Woe to the apostate and his zodiac constellation* [*mazal*]. There is no curse against Christendom mentioned in these words. It is, as mentioned above, a reference to the future, that the Holy One will make the mountains and valleys equal. He will make it dark before the Day of Judgment for all people, as Ezekiel 38 says:

Ezekiel 38. "*They shall quake before Me, etc. . . . mountains shall be overthrown, cliffs shall topple, and every wall shall crumble to the ground*" [Ezekiel 38:20]. Everything in this chapter refers to Gog and Magog.

Isaiah 40. Also, Isaiah 40. "*Every hill and mountain made low*" [Isaiah 40:4]. I can interpret the mountains literally, or as a parable about the mighty kings and lords. This path is followed by the liturgical poets, that before the Day of Judgment everything will become similar and unified, as the verse says, "*The whole country shall become like the Aravah, etc.*" [Zechariah 14:10]. "*All the nations will be covered by fog.*" All the nations will be covered by fog.

The liturgical poet has this from the verse, "*Behold, darkness shall cover the earth*" [Isaiah 60:2].

Isaiah 60.

See in Ezekiel and Zechariah what will happen before the Day of Judgment. Our prayers address this, but we do not curse anyone, and it does not refer to any Christian.

Ezekiel 38 and 39, end of Zechariah.

12

Now the apostate brings the memorial book from the Sabbath where we say, "*May God remember the souls,*" and says that we name dukedoms, earldoms, kingdoms, and imperial cities. We pray that the Holy One should punish them before our eyes, like Sodom and Gomorrah, and the people shout "amen." I say that we do pray that the Holy One should remember the souls of the martyrs and should be gracious to them because of the troubles they suffered, and allow their merit to benefit us. We remember and pray for our deceased ancestors who were not killed, and we give charity for the sake of their souls. We do not wish the rulers any ill, since the majority of the evil decrees occurred against the will of the rulers [and were perpetrated] by the ordinary people.[14] They are no longer alive. Why should the Christians who are alive be responsible for the deeds of their ancestors who lived many hundreds of years ago? It is written, "*Parents shall not be put to death for children, nor children be put to death for parents*" [Deuteronomy 24:16]. His son the apostate has responded falsely.

The apostate writes that we pray every Sabbath that the Christians should be annihilated, like Sodom and Gomorrah.

13

Now the apostate writes that we jump toward the moon and say, "*May Your anxiety and fear fall upon them, etc.*" This means God should throw anxiety and fear upon the Christians. I call upon the testimony of the

14. This is a reference to the *Av ha-Rahamim* prayer recited on Sabbath mornings in memory of the martyrs of the Crusades and other persecutions and deceased members of the community. His argument is that the evil deeds were opposed by the rulers and perpetrated by the mobs of ordinary people.

prayer. Just as I jump before the moon and cannot reach it, so too my enemies should not be able to reach me to do evil. We mean enemies but not Christians who do not do anything to us. We consider them to be friends.[15]

14

How the apostate translates "to the apostates."

The apostate writes further that we pray in the *Shemoneh Esreh*, "*May there be no hope for the apostates, etc.*" This means there should be no hope for the baptized Jews and the Christians. They should all be destroyed in the blink of an eye. Concerning this I present a long introduction *in the book that I prepared for the Christians*. I say that no Christians are intended here, but only *minim*; these are heretics and Sadducees. However, what is meant by "apostate," how it is translated, and how Ramban translates it is written above.[16] This is someone who is estranged; one who makes himself a stranger. He does everything. Does he not know the Torah of Moses? He denies his laws, as mentioned above. A Jew who commits only one transgression, he is called an apostate [*meshumad*] to that transgression, as mentioned above.

How Zalman Zvi of Aufhausen translates "apostate," and why the majority have themselves baptized.

How I, Zalman Zvi, understand "apostate" and interpret it. I will also tell you how I translate the blessing. I want to tell you that it is known that fewer than one in a hundred change their religion. One who has done some villainy or wants to do so [becomes an apostate]. Daily experience shows that the heretics or apostates [*mumarim* or *meshumadim*] thrive in Germany like the citrons in Moscow. (This is not said against all baptized Jews.) One cannot suffer the heavy laws and gladly eat pork. The second one does not want to pay tolls.[17] The third one does not tolerate that he is called derogatory names. The fourth lusts after a Christian woman or hates his wife. Through this he thinks he will be rid of his wife and get another one. So these have themselves baptized. The Christians become tired of them, since they manifest before them some of the same strange inability to fit in. One sees that they are not to be trusted, so they want to cover themselves by slandering us. They make books and satires against us to show that they are good Christians and enemies of the Jews.

---

15. This paragraph refers to the *Sanctification of the New Moon*, and the quotations are taken from this prayer.

16. *Theriak* 2.29.

17. Special tolls to enter cities levied only on Jews.

They want to make us hateful in Christian eyes, so that we would be expelled and chased away. This is their intent and hope. Therefore, we pray to God thusly, *and to the apostates there should be no hope*. The hopes of the baptized Jews should not advance (however, we do not curse them), and all heretics should be destroyed in the blink of an eye. If we had wanted to curse them, we could have said it more briefly and written, "*And the apostates and heretics should be destroyed in a moment.*" We do not curse them; they need no curses. I say that the majority of them behave badly. As soon as they deny the Jewish faith, they no longer have a place according to Jewish law. Later, when they run away to Constantinople or Venice and declare themselves as Jews, they deny the Christian law. Both laws are robbed in this way. They are proper apostates and condemned by both laws. So I describe it for myself. They desire the old law of their ancestors and to destroy us. Therefore, they are apostates. Yet not all of them are like this, as mentioned above.

The apostates hope to destroy the Jews; therefore we should pray that their hopes not be fulfilled.

And the apostates' [prayer] is recited in many places. This is against the informers. It applies to many baptized Jews, because they want to betray us by force, like this apostate and others like him. *It is enough about this here. I have expanded on this matter in the book for Christians.*

The prayer against the apostates is recited in the *Shemoneh Esreh* in many places.

15

As has been mentioned above, and as will be written about further on, we pray for their majesties, emperors, kings, and rulers. The "*wanton kingdoms.*" These are those who are wantonly cast up to become a king or emperor and are not rightfully born to it. These should be quickly uprooted, broken, shattered, and become submissive.

In the year 1338 of the Christian calendar, a rebel or wanton person named Armleder cast himself up to be a king and misled many people and started a war.[18] A penitential poem was written about this. There is a rhymed stanza in it that is as follows: "*Quickly the thicket and pestilent nations; our rulers, lords of soldiers, quickly overcome, quickly destroy the wanton kingdom.*" So you see how we pray for the rulers, against the rebels and insurgents who are called "the wanton kingdom."

1338: A rebel cast himself up to become emperor. He was called Armleder.

18. On the Armleder uprising, see *Encyclopedia Judaica*, vol. 3, 483–84.

16

Now the apostate comes to mock the prayer that says, "*Blessed are You O Lord, King of the universe, who has not made me a gentile* [*goy*]."[19] This means that we praise God that he did not make us a Christian.

Anthonius Margaritha, Martin Luther. The apostate Anthonius Margaritha and Martin Luther both translate *goy* as "heathen." What is the connection of this prayer that was instituted in the time of Ezra to a Christian? What should it be, since we also pray, "*who has not made me a woman*"? If so, it would be just for our wives to leave us. Each person rejoices and thanks God for his faith and creation.

17

The apostate further says that we pray every day, "*The Lord delivered Israel this day, etc.*" [Exodus 14:30]. It also says there, "*Terror and dread descend upon them, etc.*" [Exodus 15:16], that God will throw fear and dread on the Christians and make them silent where they stand.[20] Thus the apostate wants to interpret it as if we are fulfilling God's command.

Deuteronomy 16; Exodus 10. "*So that you may remember the day of your departure from the land of Egypt, etc.*" [Deuteronomy 16:3]. "*That you may recount in the hearing of your sons and your sons' sons, etc.*" [Exodus 10:2]. Thus the Holy One commanded us to retell every day how the Holy One led us out of Egypt.

Exodus 14. Thus we recite every day, "*The Lord delivered us*" [Exodus 14:30] and the *Song of the Sea*,[21] as they were written in the Torah several thousand years before the birth of Christianity. The rogue further lies and says that we curse the Christians with this. *There is no need to continue at length; I have discussed it at length in the book for the Christians.*

18

Now the apostate comes to the end of the *Shemoneh Esreh*. In "*May God guard my tongue from evil,*"[22] it says, "*upset their design.*" He translates it as,

19. A prayer that is part of the daily morning liturgy.
20. These verses are taken from the section of the daily prayers called the *Song of the Sea*.
21. Exodus 15:1–19.
22. The opening words of the prayer that ends the *Amidah*. The Hebrew passages are taken from this prayer.

"God will disrupt the counsel and thoughts of Christendom," and we all say "amen" to this. So I say that the ignoramus should open his eyes. This is not why it says, "*May my soul be silent to those who insult me.*" This means, "Make silent those who curse my soul." *Those who plan evil against me*, and all those who think about doing evil to me, speedily upset their designs and hinder their thoughts. This refers both to Jew and Christian. So one says this silently, and it is not a blessing, and "amen" is not said at its end. This curse falls on the apostate *who thinks evil against us and others like him*, but not against any Christian who does not harm us.

19

Now the apostate jumps to the prayers for *Rosh Hashanah*. We say: "*All the evil should be consumed like the smoke is consumed.*" This is supposed to mean: "The godless Christians should all melt away like the smoke, so that they will no longer have any authority." *Here I have explained at length in the book for the Christians* that no Christian is intended here. It is also no prayer but a story of how the end of time will be, and how the prayer-book says, "*And then the righteous will see, and they will rejoice, etc.*" See in the festival prayerbook that the apostate is a liar. We pray that the whole world should recognize God, Blessed be He.

20

The apostate writes further that between *Rosh Hashanah* and *Yom Kippur* we have horrendous prayers with which we curse the Christians. He would rather not write at length about them. *He answered falsely with this.* The apostate and his supporters do not understand a word in the [prayerbook].

The apostate writes that we pray that God should break the "*bintnus*" of the godless Christians.

He writes that we pray that *the garment of evil should be cut off.* This is translated as: "God will destroy the '*bintnus*'" of the godless Christians. I never saw or heard such a word in the prayers in all my days. Also, his own words cannot be a curse on Christians. It is a "*bintnus*" that is destroyed, not a Christian.

21

The apostate writes that we pray, "*Pour out from Your wrath.*" This means, the Christians frighten us; pour out Your wrath, etc., since You are despised among the Christians. It was written in the liturgical hymn for the third day after Rosh Hashanah that we used to recite in the past in

Ashkenaz. However, it does not say "*my wrath.*" This would be the one who frightens me. It is written "*Your wrath.*" These are those who despise You. These are those who act against God but not Christians. However, the apostates who knew nothing muttered about it, so we did not print it. One also does not pray it.

22

The apostate writes that we silently curse the Christians.

The apostate writes further that it is written in the festival prayerbook, "*because of the many troubles and impatience, etc.*" This is translated as, "The troubles that we Jews suffer; blame them on the unclean Christians. Paint your arrow in their blood. Sharpen your sword in their gullet. The kites and birds will be satiated. Let such punishments and Your fearsome wrath soon come upon the Christians." I say that the apostate writes such falsehoods, *because of the many troubles and impatience.* We should not curse a heathen, much less a Christian.

Christians call the Antichrist "Gog and Magog."

He must have found in an old book how the Holy One will throw hail and thunderstones on the bystanders and nations in the days of Gog and Magog, whom the Christians call the Antichrist. The birds and kites will be satiated with their blood and flesh, as Ezekiel and Isaiah write.

Ezekiel 39; Isaiah 34.

This refers to the resurrection of the dead or the Day of Judgment. However, we do not curse any person in our prayers.

23

The apostate writes further. We pray, "*Modu goyim yahumu, etc.*,"[23] and he translates this as, "At times we curse the Christians." This refers to the resurrection of the dead. Then the nations will boast.

Psalms 46.

In Psalms, "*Nations rage, kingdoms topple, etc.*" [Psalms 46:7]. This means, when the Holy One will raise His voice on the Day of Judgment in the valley of Jehoshaphat, as Joel writes,

Joel, end.

"God will shout down from heaven. Then the nations will growl, and the kingdoms will fall apart. They will all come and wage war against Jerusalem, and the earthly kingdoms will end."[24]

---

23. A garbled version of Psalms 46:7.
24. A reference to Joel, chapter 4.

And Zechariah writes, "*And the Mount of Olives will split, and one half shall shift, etc.*" [Zechariah 14:4]. **Zechariah, end.**

As Ezekiel writes, "*Mountains shall be overthrown, etc.*" [Ezekiel 38:20]. **Ezekiel 38.** The liturgical poets put these prophesies in the festival prayerbook. With this, the wonders that God will do on the Day of Judgment will be told. However, we wish no curses on any nation. The poem, from which the apostate selected the stanza "*nations rage,*" has forty-four stanzas. They all end with the word *kingdom* and tell how the Holy One will be King in the end of days. He will be recognized and accepted by all the nations. This is a prayer for the whole world and not a curse.

24

We pray two times every day: "*Therefore, we hope to You, Lord our God, etc.*"[25] In this we pray that the Holy One will soon cause all flesh to call His name, and all nations will call God their Lord, and there will be one faith. I have diligently translated the "*Therefore*" in the book that I wrote for the Christians.

25

The reason superfluous and spiteful things are in the festival prayerbooks.

The apostate writes that we have loathsome prayers that we should not print, and we leave them as superfluous or spiteful things with which one can blaspheme. As I heard, it was in the past that a prayer was there because of the heathens, but it did not refer to Christians. It was interpreted to our detriment, so we left it out. However, why do these spiteful or superfluous things remain? Regarding this we must give the testimony of the printers and typesetters. If we have to leave something out, then we cannot continue typesetting. We must leave the superfluous in, since we have to continue with the numbers and rows, just as the other book begins. Otherwise it would be much work and require a new arrangement of the amount [of text] and numbering [of pages]. One who understands printing gave me this testimony.[26]

---

25. This is the beginning of the second paragraph of the *Alenu* prayer, which ends each of the three daily prayer services.
26. Zalman Zvi is referring to printing a new edition of a book. If one does not follow precisely the layout of the previous edition, then a great deal of work would be required to reset the type and page layout for the entire book.

26

The apostate writes that the portion of remembrance is the Sabbath before Passover; we say, "May his name and memory be blotted out" against Jesus the Nazarene.

The ignoramus apostate writes further that the Sabbath before Passover is called *the portion of remembrance*, which is actually the Sabbath before *Purim*, on which we talk about Amalek and Haman. The apostate says that we shout out, "May his name and memory be blotted out," and we mean with this the acronym Jesus, and we pray that his name be wiped out.[27] It is well known that the whole prayer of the portion of remembrance talks about Amalek. Because it is written, "*Remember what Amalek did to you*" [Deuteronomy 25:17], about this we say, "*May his name and memory be blotted out.*" "*May his name and memory be blotted out*" is written in Polish prayerbooks. The reason why we curse him and do not remember him is written immediately afterward: "*Because he did not remember, etc.*" [Psalms 109:16]. Because this Amalek was not sensible and did not heed the miracles and wonders that the Holy One did for His people when they went out of Egypt, and he wantonly attacked us, though we had done nothing to him. Therefore the Holy One swore to wipe out his name.

Exodus 17, God wants to destroy Amalek.

Exodus 17. We pray that the Holy One should completely erase his name. The Lord, blessed be He, commanded us to always remember what he did to us.[28]

Deuteronomy 25.

Deuteronomy 25, "*Remember what Amalek did to you*" [Deuteronomy 25:17]. Because Haman was a descendant of Amalek and wanted to destroy us, we pray the Sabbath before *Purim*, not the Sabbath before Passover, as the apostate writes. We read in the Torah the portion relating to Amalek. Thus the whole liturgical poem speaks about Amalek. What should I write about what happens on that day? *The truth will make its own path.* We do not think ill of Yeshua the Nazarene.

***Megillah*, page 18.**

See in tractate *Megillah*, page 18[a]. All the reasons why we should be opposed to Amalek forever are cited there. *I have expanded in the book for the Christians.*

27

The apostate writes further. We give the Christians gruesome curses that are in the *portion of remembrance. We say: "God should give the vengeance*

27. The Hebrew phrase is *yemakh shemo ve-zikhro*. If one takes the first letter of each word, the resulting acronym spells *Yeshu*, the Hebrew name for Jesus.
28. Exodus 17:14.

against Edom into our hands."[29] This means, God should account to the Christians, and even more curses. *He has responded falsely against us.* This is written nowhere. Rather, "*He will give the vengeance against His enemies into our hands.*"[30] This means, to His enemies (these are the Amalekites, against whom God swore to fight and to destroy them), God should give His accounting and vengeance through our hands. We do not mention any Christians. The apostate also wants to call the Christians "Edomites." Wherever "Edomite" is written, it does not refer to Christians. Christians are not Edomites and also will not become them.

Ezekiel has called out all the nations. He uses these words, "to the Edomites, Philistines, and other nations."[31] However, our prayer curses no Christians. **Ezekiel 25.**

28

Now the apostate comes again to "*their kingdom.*" I have responded to this above, that it all refers to the Day of Judgment. **Paragraph 25.**

29

Now the apostate moves from *Yom Kippur* to Passover and gives a contemptible *Seder*. He says that we say: "*Pour out Your wrath on the kingdoms who do not call Your name*" [Jeremiah 10:25]. He leaves out "*who do not know You*" [Jeremiah 10:25]. He translates the verse: "*Pour out Your wrath on the Christians and on the kingdoms that do not know and praise You.*"

Look at the apostate liar and ignoramus. The verses found in Psalms 79 and Jeremiah 10 were written more than a thousand years before the birth of Christianity. It is explicitly written, "Pour out Your wrath on the nations who do not know You, and on the kingdoms who do not call Your name." The psalm speaks solely about the nations who were idol-worshipers. It begins, "*O God, heathens have entered Your domain, etc.*" [Psalms 79:1]. However, why do we recite the verse on Passover? This is because we are speaking about the redemption from Egypt and Pharaoh, who said, "*Who is the Lord . . . ? I do not know the Lord, etc.*" [Exodus 5:2]. "Who is God that I should listen to His voice, I do not know God?" Concerning **Psalms 79; Jeremiah, end of 10; pour out Your wrath on the nations.**

---

29. This is a rewriting of Ezekiel 25:14. In Ezekiel God speaks in the first person.
30. This is not a Biblical verse.
31. Ezekiel 25:12–17.

this we say, "*Pour out Your wrath.* Pour out Your wrath on the nations who do not know You, etc." We mean with this, Pharaoh, king of Egypt, and others like him, and not the Christians. They call to God and know Him. See in the *Sefer Ma'aseh Adonai*, written by Rabbi Eliezer, of blessed memory,[32] who cites many things concerning the verse "*Pour out Your wrath*" [Psalms 79:6]. *I have written at length in the book that I made for the Christians and I have cited everything. Here, there is no need, only the falsehoods of the apostate, which are lies and fallacies.*

30

The apostate writes again that we leave superfluous and spiteful things in books where we curse and blaspheme against Christians. I have responded to this above in paragraph 25, why the printers leave spiteful things.

31

The year 5352, the press in Tannhausen in Swabia.

The apostate writes further that in the year 1592 of the Christian calendar, that is five thousand and three hundred and fifty-two years since the creation of the world, they printed festival prayerbooks in Tannhausen in Swabia.[33] The ruler closed the press because they found curses and blasphemies in it. Rogues like the apostate reported this to the ruler, but they found that it was false, and they again allowed them to follow the festival prayerbooks. They can still be found in all areas of Ashkenaz. I, Zalman Zvi, have a copy of this printing. The apostate brings this falsehood, which uncovers his dirt and lies, and brings our innocence into the light of day. "*Dirt should be put in the mouth of that person*";[34] "*He who speaks untruth shall not stand before my eyes*" [Psalms 101:7]. Enough of the fifth chapter.

---

32. *Sefer Ma'aseh Adonai* is a commentary on the Torah written by Rabbi Eliezer Ashkenazi (1513–86). It was first published in Venice (1583).
33. Concerning this work and its history, see Joseph Perles, "Bibliographische Mittheilungen aus München," *Monatsschrift für Geschichte und Wissenschaft des Judentums* 25 (1876): 350–51.
34. B. *Baba Bathra* 16a. An expression meaning "he should be silenced."

CHAPTER 6

Herein is announced that the apostate from Oettingen understands nothing in the Talmud, and that the *aggadot* are not to be understood literally. Also, that he does not know the Christian Gospels, nor has he read them.

1

First, I have no reason in the sixth chapter to respond very much to the apostate from Oettingen, since for the most part he brings *aggadot* with which he wants to ridicule us and strengthen his faith with this. We were not very interested in this, since he did not attack us so strongly in the previous five chapters. He accused us of all the evil things, and it did not bother me or any other Jew. However, regarding what I wrote against him, I had an urgent need to rescue the honor of all Jews; foremost, to change the opinion about the Holy Torah, and I might call my refutation a "principal text." This is a response and a protection from the enemy.

However many of the *aggadot* in the Talmud one comes across are not simple to understand as they are written. They have esoteric and unusual interpretations, since all the prophets and sages relayed their wisdom through parables, and the ordinary people cannot understand them. The apostate in his *Schlangenbalg* wants to force them into a narrow interpretation, even though similar things are found many times in the Christian Gospels.

***Aggadot* of the Talmud cannot be understood according to their literal meaning.**

Yeshua the Nazarene spoke in parables many times.

Yeshua the Nazarene spoke in parables and allegories.

Even his students and disciples could not understand them and had to ask him, as it says many times in Matthew, Mark, and Luke.

Matthew 13; Mark 4; Luke 8.

Matthew 13.

In the same day, Jesus left the house and sat down by the sea. Many people gathered around him, and he spoke about various things to them through parables. He said: "A sower went out to sow, etc."[1]

This weed is an explanation of some baptized Jews who want to number themselves among the pious Christians, like the apostate Samael Friedrich.

Now he presented another parable before them and said: "The kingdom of heaven is like a person who sows good seeds in his furrows. However, when the people are sleeping, his enemy comes and sows weeds among the wheat, etc."[2]

Another parable in Mark 4; Luke 13. He presents to them and says that the kingdom of heaven is like a mustard seed.[3] Another parable, the kingdom of heaven is like yeast.[4] Jesus described all this through parables. Yeshua the Nazarene spoke through parables many times in the Gospels, and his students had to ask what he meant. He expounded it in this way. The apostate ridicules the Talmud when he talks about *aggadot* by way of parable. There are a number of books of Midrash and commentaries on the *aggadot*. Also, the majority of the *aggadot* that he cites were written very differently. Some of them are complete lies. He never studied or understood one word in the Talmud in his whole life. Apostate, *what do you have to do with aggadah, go to tractate Negaim*?[5] I have to recount one thing that he wrote. There was a rabbi in the Talmud who said that the Messiah would ride on an ass, as Zechariah writes.[6]

Zechariah, "*humble, riding on an ass.*"

Another rabbi said: "This is a disgrace, to ride on a donkey. If I knew when the Messiah was supposed to come, I would have sent him a fine-colored horse that was worth one hundred thalers." The liar presents this Talmudic passage not as it was written, and he does not name the rabbis.

***Sanhedrin* 98.**

It is written in [tractate] *Sanhedrin*, "*Rabbi Joshua ben Levi said, etc.*" Once it is written, the Messiah will arrive on a cloud. In another place it is

1. Matthew 13:3.
2. Matthew 13:24–25.
3. Mark 4:30–31; Luke, 13:18–19.
4. Luke 13:20–21.
5. B. *Hagigah* 14a. This is a Talmudic phrase used as a rebuke to someone who comments on esoteric topics when he does not have the knowledge or understanding of these matters. Tractate *Negaim* deals with ritual purity; its focus is at the opposite end of the intellectual spectrum from mystical and esoteric matters.
6. Zechariah 9:9.

written that he would arrive on an ass. There is no difference between them. When Israel will be pious, he will arrive on a cloud in majesty. If they will not be pious, then he will arrive humbly, on an ass. Concerning this, King Shapur (this was a Persian king, not a rabbi, as the apostate writes) said:

He will at least arrive on an ass.

"You say that he will arrive on an ass. If I knew when, I would send him my official or personal horse." He said this mockingly. Concerning this, Rabbi Joshua said again, but by way of vexation: "*Do you have one of one hundred colors*? This means, dear one, do you have a horse that has one hundred colors, like the ass will have on which the Messiah will ride?"[7] Thus, the apostate ignoramus spoke about the color like a blind man. He translated one hundred colors as one hundred thalers, and King Shapur, king of Persia, as a rabbi. If the apostate were an ass, he could be ridden like Balaam's ass. Then he would speak better and more truthfully than his brothers, the asses. *However, all of his words are foolish falsehoods and lies.*

2

The apostate writes that we say that the Torah teaches that we should kill a Christian who studies Torah.

Now the apostate writes that it is written in the Talmud. A rabbi said that when a Christian studies Torah in the Five Books of Moses, then one should publicly kill him. However, he doesn't write where and in which tractate this was written. It does say: "*A gentile who engages in Torah study is punishable by death.*[8] This is a heathen idol-worshiper who studies the Five Books of Moses. He is punishable by the death penalty because he studies the Torah only to ridicule it and to destroy it. He considers it a poem and a lie. Therefore, he is punishable by the death penalty. God will kill him. However, it is not to be understood that we should kill him. We should not kill anyone. Whenever it says "punishable by death" in the Talmud, it is understood as death at the hands of heaven.

"Punishable by the death penalty" is death at the hands of heaven.

This is death at the hands of heaven. God shortens his life; he dies before his time. However, a Christian who believes that the Law of Moses is proven and what is written in it is true, and does not study it to ridicule it, then they do right to study it. We ourselves teach the Christians. *I have expanded on this in the book that I wrote for the Christians*, that Jews are lecturers in colleges.

---

7. B. *Sanhedrin* 98a.
8. B. *Sanhedrin* 59a.

Elia Bahur, author of the grammar. The Christians study his books.

Elia Bahur wrote the best grammar; this is his book on grammar. The Christians study his books. He taught in Rome and Venice.[9]

***Baba Kamma*, page 38.**

I have shown above that [tractate] *Baba Kamma* and tractate *Avodah Zarah* write: "A heathen who studies Torah and studies the Law of Moses, he is as good as the high priest."[10] Thus anyone who studies the Law and does not ridicule it, he is an honest person and is highly honored. It is the same, whether Christian or Jew. How should we, heaven forbid, kill him? *Would that God cause that the whole world* would know the Torah. The whole world would, as mentioned above, learn Torah before the Day of Judgment. *His son the apostate responds with falsehoods.*

Maimonides, at the end of his book.

Maimonides writes that the heathens should be warned that they should not study the Law, because they wanted to mock it. When they will not study for God's sake but want to study in order to mock, the Holy One would punish them, and shorten their lives. However, nobody should kill them, whether Christian, heathen, or Turk. The person should not take the life that God gives. It happens through the judgment and law of God and their majesties, the rulers.

3

The Written Torah of Moses is the *Gemara*, and the Gemara is the Torah of Moses.

The apostate writes that we rely more on the Talmud than on the Written Torah of Moses, and whoever does not rely on the Talmud is called a heretic. True, we rely on one as much as we rely on the other, since the Talmud is a gloss, commentary, and exposition of the Written Torah, as has been demonstrated above.

The Talmud interprets: Ammonite and not Ammonitess; Moabite and not Moabitess. The Christians themselves have to recognize this, that the Written Torah needs exegesis. They were both given at Sinai. Whichever Jew questions the Oral Torah, which is the Talmud, or does not observe it, is a heretic, and also questions the Written Torah. Therefore we bring evidence and proofs from the Talmud in this book.

9. Elijah Levita wrote a number of important books on Hebrew grammar. Most likely this is a reference to his book *Sefer ha-Bahur* (Rome, 1519). The basic study of his life and work is G. E. Weil, *Elie Levita: Humaniste et massorete (1469–1549)* (Leiden: Brill, 1963). See also Deena Aranoff, "Elijah Levita: A Jewish Hebraist," *Jewish History* 23 (2009): 17–40.

10. B. *Baba Kamma* 38a.

It orders us that we should not kill or deceive anyone, engage in magic, or engage in dishonest business. We should give charity to Jews and gentiles, not curse anyone, honor the rulers, pray for their welfare and peace. Whoever does not follow this denies both Torahs and is not a Jew.

What the Talmud teaches the Jews.

Now the apostate claims that we call the Sadducees or those who mock the Talmud heretics. Above, he said that we call the Calvinists or Zwingliites[11] heretics. Heaven forbid. Here one can grasp his lies.

Now the apostate says that we call the Sadducees heretics. Above, he said that we call Calvinists heretics.

4

The apostate writes further. The Talmud writes: "*Three are impudent. They are Israel among the nations, the dog among animals, the rooster among fowl.*"[12] He also says that we confess that we are insolent. I admit that we are impudent, but we are not insolent; rather we are steadfast in our beliefs. We are faithful and beloved like a dog that faithfully obeys his master, courageous to serve him faithfully in the middle of the night, to protect what is his. He enjoys any small or ordinary thing that is thrown to him. If he is hit on the nose, he comes again when his master says a good word to him, and forgets everything that has been done to him previously. The Jew is as sensitive as the dog. He searches here and there with his means and through business brings game and all other things to his master's kitchen. For this he is given some broth to slurp as a reward. A dog must lie outside the door or the pen. The poor Jewish dog has to pay a toll in all the cities ruled by the German nation (though not in Italy or Poland). He gives everyone joy, but there is none for him. A dog[13] that eats something; one comes and thrashes him. He must sweat because he had eaten something.[14] When a Jew engages in a little usury (he must nourish himself from this, as all other handcrafts and agriculture are forbidden to him), if he takes too much for himself, he is punished and oppressed and must return twice as much. A dog often has his bone torn from his mouth and must sleep with a hungry stomach. So the baptized Jews like Samael Friedrich and others like him come and also take from us the poor usury. They are Christians, eat

Why Jewish law is compared to dogs; a nice discourse.

---

11. Followers of Huldrych Zwingli (1484–1531), a leader of the Reformation in Switzerland.
12. B. *Bezah* 25b.
13. This is an extended metaphor for how the Jews were treated.
14. He sweats in anxiety that he might be beaten again for having eaten something.

pork, and take usury like Jews, as is described above. So I must suffer much, because I am called a Jewish dog. No Jew has yet spoken angrily to me. *I have expanded on this in the book that I prepared for the Christians.* Enough of the apostate's lies. *I have faith in the God who created the mountains.*

CHAPTER 7

1

In the seventh and last chapter, the apostate wants to prove that our Talmud itself writes against our faith, and he writes that the Christian faith is correct. I say, whichever way you look at it, who were the Talmudic rabbis? They were Jews. Why would they have written that the Christian faith was correct? Were they fools that they would write publicly against their faith? Were they Christians? Why did they believe so much in Judaism and write against other religions (as the apostate himself writes)? Why did they not quickly and publicly accept the Christian faith? I myself say and confess to all Christians that the Talmudic rabbis were good Jews, and the majority of the things the apostate writes are false, and he did not understand a word. He pilfered from the books of other apostates. He says that the Talmud admits that God is one in substance and threefold in person. He describes how a rabbi dreamed that he heard a voice from heaven that said to him: "I, you, and your disciples have been called to the Trinity." The fool heard someone reading [tractate] *Hagigah*, that seven groups sit before the Holy One, and the rabbi was listed in the third group; that he would sit in the same group in the Garden of Eden.[1] The fool translated "third group" as "trinity." I might have tolerated it if he had only cited such foolishness and had not abused the Jews. How much effort and work would I have missed and writing would I have saved? Now I have had this book printed in the Latin alphabet, hoping that many honest Christians of high and low station will desire good for the Jews.

The apostate writes that the Talmud writes against the Jewish faith.

1. B. *Hagigah* 14b.

Why Zalman had this book printed in the Latin and Hebrew alphabets.

I had this book printed in Yiddish in the Hebrew alphabet so that someone will know how to respond to Christians in conducive circumstances, and also to understand from this and keep in mind what a great sin it is to deceive a Christian, with words or deeds. God recognizes and rewards me, my poor wife, and children, temporally and eternally, for my faithful opinions, efforts, and work, with a plea and a desire that one should accept it with love. Nobody should take it amiss or be angry with me if I have missed something. They should have compassion on me, my wife, and my children, and they should take to heart how long they were in hunger and need. I had to leave out whole sections of the book. They should consider that I must have a bite to eat in order to print the Latin alphabet version. If someone would be a sponsor or a partner for the book, he should give more than he expected; good things will come to him from God and from the world. This is something new *that never existed before*, and nobody who reads through it will be offended. With this I will find luck, healing, peace, and all welfare, *in the eye of every reader, in this world and in the world that is completely good. Our God should give us the merit to see the comforting of Zion and the rebuilding of Jerusalem, amen. So desires your servant*, Zalman Zvi Aufhausen, *for every reader.*

Tuesday, *Rosh Hodesh Nisan*, in the year ShLoMo"H [1615], in the small counting.

List of the Apostate's Accusations

With this, everyone can see what the apostate from Oettingen suspects ordinary Jews of, and what he had printed in his book called *Schlangenbalg*. I have noted them in numerical order and responded to all the points with truth, as you will find in this book.

CHAPTER 1

1. They call Christ *tola*. This means one who was hanged and an evildoer.
2. They call him "Yeshua the Nazarene." This means the worst and despised.
3. They call Christ *an illegitimate [mamzer], son of a menstruant* [*nidah*]. This means, the son of a whore, who was in impurity.
4. When one Jew despises and derides another Jew, he says, "You Jesus the Nazarene."
5. When someone wants to do something not good, they say to him, "You Jesus the Nazarene, you hanged one."
6. They say that God ordered Jesus to go to Rome and say that he was not the Messiah. Thus he should not be persecuted anymore. Also, when somebody wakes up early, they say, "You woke up before the hanged one has visited."
7. The apostate writes further about a book that is supposedly called *Ma'aseh Tolah*. He repeats great foolishness and falsehoods.
8. Jews say Yeshua the Nazarene stole the Ineffable Name [*Shem ha-Meforash*] from the Temple. The apostate writes much foolishness about why the Christian priests wear tonsures.
9. Why do they not sweep the synagogue in Worms?

The title "List of the Apostate's Accusations" is found only on the running heads for this section in the original text; it does not appear as a formal section title.

10. Jews wake up the day after Yom Kippur in the name of Satan.
11. Jews make tables levitate through magic.
12. Jews invoke the Queen of Sheba through magic and dance with her.
13. Jews cause a lump of clay to live through incantations so that it moves.
14. Jews put an apple in the hands of the dead on which is written devils' names, and with this they kill Christians.
15. Jews kill women in childbirth and their children with magic.
16. Jews write amulets for women in childbirth, probably with Christian blood.
17. Jews believe that anything they do to Christians is not a sin.
18. Jews say that those who acquire the world to come are those who keep quiet and deny the blocked[1] Christian god. Also, as in the year 1582, a Jew in Dietenheim died under torture, sanctifying the Name of God.
19. Jews lament together that the hanged murdered one is not forgotten.
20. Jews eat garlic on Christmas night to dishonor Christ, and they say that Yeshua the Nazarene crawls out of all the mouse holes and corners on this night.

CHAPTER 2

1. Jews call the mother of Yeshua the Nazarene an impure adulteress and whore.
2. They call their festival "*trefah* hanged one's festival," which means "unclean gallows celebration"; and the disciples of Yeshua the Nazarene, "the *trefah* hanged one's *trefah students who fall into bad ways*," [which means] "the unclean, damned, hanged one's disciples."
3. They call the celebrations of the students of the Nazarene "the *trefah* student's holiday." This means "the unclean, damned disciples' celebration."
4. They call the Lutheran preachers "*trefah* teachers of falsehood." This means, "the unclean false teachers."
5. They call the pope *apifior*, a mocking, despicable name.
6. A cardinal, "an elector pauper."[2]
8. A bishop, "a hegemon." Canons, "unclean nobles."
9. The Crusaders, "*trefah* cross nobles."
10. An abbot, "priest." An abbess, a "priestess." A nobleman, "*a lunatic.*" A noblewoman, "*female lunatic.*" These are noble, mocking, and despicable names.

---

1. "Blocked" here is the Yiddish term often used for "uncircumcised."
2. Number 7 is missing from the list. This is perhaps a printer's error.

11. They call a schoolmaster "*trefah* foolish-master."
12. Town and magistrate's clerks, "*kofer*." This is one who denies God.
13. They call the popish faith "the old evil faith."
14. The Lutherans, "the new evil faith."
15. They call the Calvinists "heretics." They are unbelievers.
16. They call the Latin language "the language of impurity, the unclean language."
17. Jews use writings with the Latin alphabet to wipe themselves, especially with the words "Yeshua the Nazarene."[3]
19. They call the churches *toevah*. This is translated as "abomination."
20. They call the church "the house of the cross and residence."
21. They call a child's baptism "the bastard's apostasy." This means a whore's child whom one destroys.
22. When they ring in the morning and evening, the Jews say that they are ringing "the *trefah gallows* bell." This means "the unclean gallows bell."
23. They call the chalice a *kelev*. This means "a dog."
24. They call mass vestments *met* vestments. This means, "death vestments."
25. We call the holy water in the baptismal font "waters of impurity."
26. Every Sabbath Jews pray for those who frustrate baptisms.
27. When someone has himself baptized, his whole family is scorned.
28. Church festivals are called *kirdol.*
29. Baptized Jews are apostates. This means "blotted out by God."
30. The Christian Eucharist is given many derisive names: "impure bread," "impure meal," "ate the hanged one," etc.
31. The Jews call the cross "idol worship," and spit on it and curse it. They disturb twigs arranged like a cross.
32. When somebody goes through a churchyard, his prayers are not heard for thirty days.
33. When a Christian swears by a sacrament, the Jew says that he has sworn by false impurity. This means by the false, unclean faith.
34. When one sees a destroyed church, Jews say, "The Holy One should destroy all churches thusly."

CHAPTER 3

1. Jews stand obediently before rulers but curse them secretly.
2. When a ruler does not allow something, it is called a "wicked kingdom."
3. The Christian advisors are called *yohazim*. They should tear themselves apart.

---

3. Number 18 is missing from the list. This is perhaps a printer's error.

4. They curse him with epilepsy.[4]
6. Christians are called "Haman," tormentor of the Jews.
7. The mayor is called "the chief uncircumcised one," "the leader of the godless ones."
8. Jews always take the Christians as an expiation.
9. On Yom Kippur Jews permit swearing falsely against Christians.
10. Jews swear by the Christian false faith.
11. Many great stories about what Jews do with usury and deceitfulness.
12. Rulers take bribes from Jews.
13. Jews do not consider adultery to be a sin.
14. Jews spit on the back half [of the animal] and wish you a poisonous death.
15. When an animal dies naturally, he gives it to the Christian as good meat.
16. Jews do not consider murder and deadly assault to be a sin.
17. In Poland and Bohemia they kill the informers and apostates. They say that this is permitted. The children should testify that the apostate was right.

CHAPTER 4

1. Christians have no greater enemies than Jews, and they do everything to the contrary.
2. When a Christian dies, the Jew says: "He has dropped dead as an expiation, and his soul is in Gehenna."
3. They say about dead Christians, "*The name of the evildoer rots.*"
4. The Jews use unheard-of curses and false words against Christians.
5. They call the Christian graves "*impure graves.*"
6. They call Christians "uncircumcised ones." These are those who do not know God.
7. They call the youths on the streets "detestable" [*shekez*].
8. Jews give Christians many curses.
9. Jews do not give charity to Christians; they wish them a bad death, bad luck, and all troubles.
10. Jews do not go out of a Christian house without taking straw or wood.
11. The Talmud teaches the Jews how to take away luck from Christians.
12. Christians are not acceptable as witnesses among Jews.
13. The Talmud writes that Christians are not people but rather animals.
14. Jews say that Christians have no marriage.

---

4. Number 5 is missing from the list. This is perhaps a printer's error.

15. When a Jew mentions a Christian, they say: "*to separate between the impure and the pure.*"
16. Jews curse the Christian cities and all the produce when they go through a city where the majority living there are Christian.
17. A Jew says to a Christian: "Too many for your eyes."
18. One should not speak with any Christian on the Sabbath.
19. On the Sabbath Jews boast about how they cheated the Christians. One should take the Christian's heart. Jews say that "he brought a sacrifice. "
20. *The best of the gentiles should be killed.*
21. When a ruler does good for the Jews, the Jew says: "This ruler does not believe in Yeshua the Nazarene."
22. Jewish physicians consider it a positive commandment to kill Christians.
23. When a *mohel* circumcises as many [infants] as [the numerical value of] his name, he has a share in the world to come.
24. Jews say that the Holy One rests on the hands of the priests, and the one who looks at this becomes blind.
25. The story of Kamza and Bar Kamza, rather than any sins, was supposed to have caused the destruction of the Temple.
26. Jews have Karaites and Sadducees among them and many diverse customs.
27. Jews can attain the world to come through excessive eating and drinking, and they have two souls on the Sabbath.[5]

CHAPTER 5

1. Jews curse Christ and all those who believe in him.
2. Jews pray, "*Zamdu be-kabzekha shashua la-tola.*"
3. Jews pray, "*Ten kevodekha la-tola.*"
4. Jews pray, "*That they bow down to nothing and emptiness.*" They changed this to Yeshua the Nazarene.
5. Jews pray, "*He should break the yoke of the nations.*"
6. "*The wicked kingdom should be speedily uprooted.*"
7. "*Destroy the evil decree of our judgment.*" This means, against Christians.
8. "*He should wage war.*" God will send war against the Christians.
9. "*Arise and carry,*" harsh curses against the Christians.
10. God should overturn the throne of Christendom.
11. Mountains and valleys should fall on the Christians.

5. Paragraph number 27 is missing from the main text; however, the material discussing this topic is found there.

12. On the Sabbath we pray for those who will disrupt baptisms.[6]
13. God should throw anxiety and fear on the Christians.
14. How the apostate translates [the prayer] "and to the apostates," and how Zalman Zvi translates it.
15. Who is the *kingdom of wickedness*?
16. "*Who has not made me a gentile.*"
17. God will cast anxiety and fear on the Christians.
18. God should disrupt the thoughts of the Christians.
19. The godless Christians should all dissolve, like smoke.
20. Jews have horrible prayers between Rosh Hashanah and Yom Kippur.
21. Jews pray, "Pour out Your wrath on the Christians."
22. God wants to avenge the Jewish suffering on the Christians.
23. Jews curse the Christians.
24. "*Therefore, we hope to You.*"
25. Jews leave superfluous things in the places where they curse Christians.
26. Jews mean Yeshua the Nazarene with "*May his name and memory be blotted out*" in the *portion of remembrance.*
27. There are great curses in the *portion of remembrance*, and they call Christians "Edom."
28. "*Their kingdom*," Jews pray against Christians.
29. "*Pour out Your wrath on the nations.*"
30. Jews leave in the superfluous.
31. Festival prayerbooks were printed in Tannhausen, Swabia.

CHAPTER 6

1. The whole chapter lays out that the apostate knows nothing about *aggadot*; nor does he understand anything in the Talmud. The apostate also never read the Christian Gospels. There are also many nice stories and parables to be found in it.
2. When a Christian studies Torah, he should be put to death publicly.
3. Jews rely on the Talmud more than they do on the Written Torah.
4. "*Three are impudent.*" A nice discussion of why Jews are compared to dogs.

CHAPTER 7

1. Lays out what the Talmudic sages said about the Messiah. The apostate lied about the Talmud and did not understand any of it.

6. There is a discrepancy between the text in chapter 5, paragraph 12, and the description that appears on this list.

APPENDIX I

Publication History of the *Schlangenbalg* and *Theriak*

JUDISCHER ABGESTREIFFTER SCHLANGEN-BALG.

NOTES

The two 1614 editions are completely identical, except for the last line, which mentions the printer and place of publication; therefore I did not reprint the text of the title page. Because the orthography of the 1680 edition is different from that of the two 1614 editions, I have also reprinted the text of the 1680 title page. Despite the minor differences in orthography, the meaning of the text is the same; thus I have provided only one English translation for the title page of the *Schlangenbalg*. I have not closely examined the complete text of the three editions of the *Schlangenbalg*. However, I did so for the editions of the *Theriak* and found them to be completely identical. I have no reason to believe that the same is not true for the editions of the *Schlangenbalg*.

I came across references to editions of the *Schlangenbalg* published in 1702 and 1716 in a number of bibliographical citations. I found copies of these two editions in the State Library in Berlin. The only connection between these two editions and Brenz's book is the title, *Judischer Schlangenbalg*. Brenz's name is not mentioned on the title page; instead of Brenz's seven chapters, this anonymous work has twenty chapters. Like Brenz's work, it claims to be an attack on the lies and blasphemies of the Jews.

EDITIONS

1. Nürnberg (1614)[1]

JUDISCHER ABGESTREIFFTER SCHLANGEN-BALG.

Dass ist:

Gründtliche entdeckung unnd verwerffung aller Lästerung und Lügen / derer sich das gifftige Judische Schlangenzifer und Otterngezicht / wider den Frömbsten / unschuldigen Juden Christum Jesum / und sein gantzes theuer ertaufftes Heiligthum / theils in den verfluchten Synagogen / theils in Häusern und heimlichen zusammenkunfften pflegt zugebrauchen.

In 7. Unterschiedliche Capitel verfasset / und zu ehrnrettung Christi Jesu dess rechten Israeliten / frommen Christen / als nun mehr meinen Brüdern unnd Schwestern am Glauben zur treuen warnung / den Jüdischen Blindschleichen zur Buss und bekehrung in Druck verfertiget

Durch

Samuel Friderich Brentzen /getaufften Juden / Gräflichen Oetingischen Dienern.

Gedruckt zu Nürmberg / durch Balthasar Scherffen / Anno 1614.

2. Augsburg (1614)[2]

The text of the title page is identical to that of the Nürnberg (1614) edition. The only difference is the last line.

Gedruckt zu Augspurg / bey Christoff Mang. 1614.

(Printed in Augsburg / by Christoff Mang. 1614.)

1. For a copy of the Nürnberg (1614) edition, see books.google.com/books?id=UBNTAAAAcAAJ&printsec=frontcover&dq=samuel+friedrich+brenz&hl=en&sa=X&ei=N8iAVJL_AYibgwT_yYHADQ&ved=0CCEQ6AEwAA#v=onepage&q=samuel%20friedrich%20brenz&f=false (last accessed August 25, 2015).
2. For the Augsburg (1614) copy in the Bavarian State Library, see www.mdz-nbn-resolving.de/urn/resolver.pl?urn=urn:nbn:de:bvb:12-bsb10903801-3 (last accessed August 25, 2015).

3. Nürnberg (1680)

JÜDISCHER ABGESTREIFFTER
SCHLANGEN-BALG /

Das ist:

Gründtliche Entdeckung und Berwerfung aller Lästerung und Lügen / derer sich das giftige Jüdische Schlangen-Geziefer und Otterngezücht / wider den Frömmsten und unschuldigen Juden Christum JESUM/ und Sein gantzes theuer ertaufftes Heiligthum / theils in den verfluchten Synagogen / theils in Häusern und heimlichen zusammenkunften pflegt zu gebrauchen.

In sieben unterschiedliche Capitel verfasset / und zu Ehren-Rettung Christi Jesu dess rechten Israeliten/ frommen Christen / als nunmehr meinen Brüdern unnd Schwestern am Glauben / zur treuen Warnung / den Jüdischen Blind-Schleichen zur Buss und Bekehrung / in Druck verfertiget

Durch

Samuel Friedrich Brentzen/getaufften Juden / und Hoch-Gräflich-Oettingischen Dienern.

Nürnberg /
Gedruckt durch Balthasar Scherfen / Anno 1614.
Daselbst zum andern mal gedruckt / bey Andreas Knorzen.
Im Jahr Christi 1680.

English translation:

JEWISH STRIPPED OFF
SNAKE-SKIN

This is:

A thorough disclosure and condemnation of all blasphemy and lies / that the poisonous Jewish snake vermin and generation of vipers / against the most pious, blameless Jewish Christian, Jesus / and his whole dear baptized Church / which they employed partially in the cursed synagogues / partially in homes and secret gatherings.

Written in seven distinct chapters / and for the vindication of Jesus Christ the true Israelite / pious Christians / who are at present my brothers and sisters in the Faith, as a sincere warning / to the Jewish serpents in the grass to repent and convert. Prepared for publication

By

Samuel Friedrich Brentz / baptized Jew / servant of the Count of Oettingen.

Nürnberg /
Printed by Balthasar Scherfen / in the year 1614.
The same, printed for the second time / by Andreas Knorzen.
In the year of Christ 1680.

4. A copy of the German text of the *Schlangenbalg* is found in *Theriaca Judaica ad Examen Revocata*, by Johann Wülfer.

YUDISHER THERIAK

EDITIONS

1. Hanau (1615)[3]

The circumstances of its publication are described in the Introduction. The title page of the Theriak, translated into English, is found at the beginning of the text translation.

2. Altdorf (1680)[4]

This edition is a copy of the Hanau (1615) edition. Page layout and pagination are the same. The Altdorf edition adds the following three lines at the bottom of the title page.

Recusum Altdorfi, Universitatis Literis,
per Henricum Meyer, Academiae Typographum.
Anno Christi M DC LXXX.

3. Nürnberg (1681)

A copy of the Yiddish text of the Theriak is found in Theriaca Judaica ad Examen Revocata, by Johann Wülfer.

4. Amsterdam (1737)[5]

Title Page. [The text is in Hebrew.]

Book of the Victory
that is called

---

3. Moritz Steinschneider, *Catalogus Librorum Hebraeorum in Bibliotheca Bodleiana* (Berlin, 1852–60), no. 6962, 1.
4. For a copy of this edition, see books.google.com/books?id=21BBAAAAcAAJ&source=gbs (last accessed August 26, 2015). Steinschneider, *Catalogus Librorum Hebraeorum in Bibliotheca Bodleiana*, no. 6962, 2.
5. Steinschneider, *Catalogus Librorum Hebraeorum in Bibliotheca Bodleiana*, no. 6962, 4.

Balm for the Jews

To close the mouth of those who unjustly open their mouth against the people of the Lord, the remnant who are dispersed and scattered to the four corners of the earth, one of the polemicists, Rabbi Zalman Zvi of Aufhausen, of blessed memory, wrote against the apostate Friedrich Brenz of Oettingen, who wickedly wrote the evil book called *Schlangen Balg* against the whole community of Israel and their remnant who did no injustice. He invented many things that were untrue. However, since the book has disappeared and is not found at all, and in particular since it was published in 1615, the learned Rabbi Sussman ben Isaac Rödelsheim, of blessed memory, was awakened and arose to publish it, editing the language so that it can be understood by everyone, and adding source notes from the Bible, Talmud, Midrashim, and other holy books. Sometimes also from books by Christian sages that were omitted by the author, of blessed memory. In order that everyone should be able to carry it in their pocket, we have printed it in a small format.

Printed in
Amsterdam

In the house of the judge, Rabbi Moses Frankfurt, may God protect him.[6]

In the year "*Is there no balm in Gilead, can no physician be found* [Jeremiah 8:22]?"[7]

5. Warsaw (1873)

NOTES

This edition, titled Merapeh Lashon (A Healing Tongue), was a Hebrew translation compiled by Abraham Kaminetsky. It does not seem to be directly related to the Amsterdam edition but is also a paraphrase and abbreviated edition of the Theriak.

TITLE PAGE

A Soothing Tongue

6. Rabbi Moses Frankfurt (or Frankfurter; 1672–1762) was an important printer and author in Amsterdam and later in Frankfurt am Main. See Jacob H. Haberman, "Moses Frankfurter," *Encyclopedia Judaica*, vol. 7 (Jerusalem: Keter, 1971), 98.
7. The year 1737 (5487) derives from the numeric Hebrew equivalence of the word "physician" and a letter in the word "balm."

A healing cure and justification of the house of Israel from the calumny of Samael Friedrich of Oettingen, who spoke and wrote against them in his book, The Elusive Serpent [Isaiah, 27:1]—Der jüdische Schlangenbalg.[8] Explained here with just proofs and trustworthy testimonies from the Bible, Mishnah, and Talmud, since all of his words are outright lies.

Which were carefully weighed and examined in the Yiddish language that was customary three hundred years ago, by one of the ancient ones, Rabbi Zalman Zvi of Aufhausen, of blessed memory, in the year 1615.

Translated into the Hebrew language by
Abraham Kaminetsky
"*A healing tongue is a tree of life, but a devious one makes for a broken spirit* [Proverbs 15:4]."
Warsaw
At the press of R. Isaac Goldman
In the year 5633 [1873], in the small counting

6. Leipzig (1882)

Max Grünbaum, in his Jüdischdeutsch Chrestomathie, devotes a chapter to the Theriak.[9] It has a brief introduction and a selection of passages from the Theriak, with brief comments.

7. New York (1928)

J. D. Eisenstein includes much of the Hebrew translation Merapeh Lashon[10] in his collection of Jewish apologetic works, Ozar Vikukhim, under the title "The Polemic of Rabbi Zalman Zvi Aufhausen Against the Apostate Friedrich Brenz."

8. Leiden Manuscript

A manuscript in the Leiden University library contains a Hebrew translation of chapter 1, paragraph 16. It is described in Moritz Steinschneider's catalog of Hebrew manuscripts in this library, listed as Ms. Warner 90 (Or. 4811).[11]

---

8. This phrase is in German Fraktur script.
9. Grünbaum, *Jüdischdeutsch Chrestomathie* (Leipzig, 1882; rep. Hildesheim: Olms, 1969), 560–85.
10. Eisenstein, *Ozar Vikukhim* (New York, 1928), 170–84.
11. Moritz Steinschneider, *Catalogus codicum hebraeorum bibliothecae academiae Lugduno-Batavae* (Leiden: Brill, 1858), 305.

THERIACA JUDAICA AD EXAMEN REVOCATA

1. Nürnberg (1681)[12]

NOTES

This work was published by Johann Wülfer (1651–1724), a Protestant theologian who lived in Nürnberg.[13] It contains the text of the Schlangenbalg, the text of the Theriak, and an extensive commentary and analysis by Wülfer. The text of the Theriak is a copy of the Altdorf (1680) edition, and the text of the Schlangenbalg is a copy of the Nürnberg (1680) edition. Wülfer's purpose was to refute Zalman Zvi's refutation of Brenz. His method was to quote a paragraph from the Theriak in the original Yiddish and then give a lengthy explanation and refutation in Latin.

TITLE PAGE

Theriaca Judaica,
ad
examen revocata,
sive
scripta amoibaea
Samuelis Friderici Brenzii, Conversi Judaei, & Salomonis Zevi,
Apellae, astutissimi, à Viris Doctis hucusque desiderata,
nunc primùm
Versione Latinà, Justisque Animadversionibus aucta,
& in publicum missa
studio
johannis wülferi.
Opus non solùm Philologis: sed & omnibus veritatis cupidis perquam utile, ac necessarium, in quo, ut Judaei plurimorum scelerum, nequitiae, & impietatis convincuntur: ita & à multis facinoribus, salvâ veritate vindicantur.

---

12. For a copy of this edition, see books.google.com/books?id=yZhLAAAAcAAJ&printsec=frontcover&dq=Theriaca+Judaica&hl=en&sa=X&ved=0CEIQ6AEwAmoVChMIr5yCvYa4xwIVjDw-Ch0EXQJ5#v=onepage&q=Theriaca%20Judaica&f=false (last accessed August 26, 2015). See also Steinschneider, *Catalogus Librorum Hebraeorum in Bibliotheca Bodleiana*, no. 6962, 3.
13. The only external information I found about Wülfer is a brief biographical entry in John McClintock and James Strong, *Cyclopedia of Biblical, Theological and Ecclesiastical Literature* (New York: Harper & Brothers, 1870).

Accessit ad calcem locupletissimus Rerum omnium Index,
&
Isaaci Vivae Vindex Sanguinis, contra Jacobum Geusium.

norimbergae
Sumtibus autoris.
Excudit Andeas Knorzius.
anno mdc. lxxxi.

APPENDIX 2

Josephus Citations in the *Theriak*

INTRODUCTION

They accuse us of every blasphemy in them. However, nobody has ventured to write against them, perhaps to please the others. Unlike our pious ones, like Josephus, who wrote against a Greek who was called Apion, and who falsely accused us Jews. He wrote fifty pages against him. You can find them in *Josephus, the Romans.* I want to follow this one and similar honest men (I have no desire to compare myself to such worthy men).

1.7

See, it is written in *Pirke Avot*, chapter 1. Simeon the Righteous was from the Great Assembly.[1] He was a member of the Great Assembly who went out of Babylon with Ezra to Jerusalem. They established our prayers. This Simeon the Righteous lived in the time of Alexander of Macedon, as Josephus writes in *Josephus, the Romans.* Josephus and Alexander of Macedon called this Simeon "Judeo," and held him in high regard, as all the chronicles write. This was one generation or period.

1.7

The Talmud also writes there that Jesus was condemned according to the laws of the Torah. He was stoned and afterward he was hanged. However Jesus of Nazareth, who was condemned under the authority of Pontius Pilate, was a healer in Jerusalem when the Romans occupied it. Yeshua the Nazarene was judged and hanged alive on the cross, which is against the laws of

1. M. *Avot* 1.2. The information he provides about these figures is not found in M. *Avot* but rather drawn from other sources.

the Torah and all Jewish practice. This is completely against Jewish law. We do not have more than the four modes of death when someone was condemned, as is written in the Torah. They are: *stoning*, *burning*, *beheading*, and *strangulation*. This means: stoning, burning, strangulation, and beheading with the sword. However, since at this time we were under the domination of the Romans, the Romans killed him on the cross while still alive, according to their practice, which under them was very cruel. Josephus writes and tells how he was once traveling and found several of his acquaintances hanging on crosses, though they were still alive, and he freed them. So we can see that the Jesus whom the Talmud writes about could not be the Christian messiah.

1.13

Josephus writes about the Essenes that they prophesied.

So too Josephus writes in his book of the Romans about the Pharisees, Sadducees, and Essenes, that the Essenes, through their seclusion, fasting, and holiness, were able to foretell the future. However, such Kabbalah is concealed from us German Jews. However, there still may be such people in the Land of Israel who can do much with this Kabbalah. However, in these lands, we do not make our golems from clay; rather they are born from the womb.

3.1.7

Josephus to *The Romans*, page 851, in the book that he wrote against Apion.

Josephus, whom the Christians call Josephus, writes in the long [book] The Romans, and many rely on it. He writes against someone called Apion, who wrote many falsehoods that they curse kings. So Yosippon writes on the meaning of the verse, "You shall not revile God, etc." [Exodus 22:27], that you should also not curse or denigrate other nations.

Josephus to *The Romans*, chapter 8, page 98.

Josephus cites many other similar proofs in chapter 8, page 98.

3.1.9

Josephus to *The Romans*, book 11, chapter 4.

Josephus to The Romans also writes this in book eleven in chapter 4.

3.1.13

Josephus, *The Jews*, book 6, chapter 77.

Josephus, The Jews, writes in book 6, chapter 47,[2] that the Jews in Asia sent a present to Hyrcanus the priest and the lords of Judah, so that they should pray for Emperor Augustus[3] and Marco Antonio of Rome.

---

2. Marginal note has 77 and the text 47.

3.1.14

Josephus, who wrote to the Romans, writes in book 2, chapter 9, how Petronio, the field commander of the emperor Gaius, desired that that his [the emperor's] image should be put in the Temple, as a remembrance. The Jews said that he should be satisfied that they prayed for him and his welfare every day in the Temple.

Josephus, *The Romans*, book 2, chapter 9

3.1.15

Josephus writes further in book 2 of Against Apion that the Jews commonly have in their custom to praise and to highly commend the emperor, the Roman empire, and people, and Jews offered sacrifices for the Romans in the Temple, etc.

Josephus writes further in *Against Apion*, book 2, that Jews pray for the Roman emperor.

3.1.16

Josephus to The Romans. Jews previously prayed in the Temple for the gentiles who were idolaters. How much more so, when we are now in exile, we pray for the Christians who are not idol-worshipers. Jews in all lands recite the blessing for their kings.

He also writes thusly about the emperor Abi Sibia in book 8, chapter 2. I would bring another hundred proofs, but enough about this. Notice, you the reader, that we blessed and prayed for the nations who worshiped the stars and constellations, who were godless heathens, and we brought sacrifices on their behalf when the Temple still stood. We also had our own kings and nobles at that time, so we did not have to do it, yet we did it. How should we Jews, now in exile, curse and denigrate the Christians?

3.12

However, you will find in Josephus, The Romans, the value of gold and silver. There is a dispute among three philosophers. One said that wine is the most valuable thing in the world. The second said a wife. The third said money.

4.25

The apostate further mocks the story of the destruction of the Temple and Kamza and Bar Kamza. The apostate says that, as a result, we have no

3. The names are set bold face in the original Yiddish text.

other reason for the destruction of the Temple. It is all because Bar Kamza was embarrassed. *I have written at length in my book for the Christians.* We say that unfortunately we committed other sins, and because of this story, Titus and Vespasian came to the Land [of Israel] and destroyed the Temple.[4]

Josephus writes how it happened.

We learn from this that nobody should embarrass his friend. However, this was not the main sin. Unfortunately, we sinned too much with other sins.

4. B. *Gittin* 55b–56a.

Bibliography

Aptroot, Marion. "Writing 'Jewish' not 'German': Functional Writing Styles and the Symbolic Function of Yiddish in Early Modern Ashkenaz." *Leo Baeck Institute Yearbook* 55 (2010): 115–28.

Aranoff, Deena. "Elijah Levita: A Jewish Hebraist." Jewish History 23 (2009): 17–40.

Arnoldi, Udo. *Pro Judaeis: Die Gutachten der hallischen Theologen im 18. Jahrhundert zu Fragen der Judentoleranz*. Berlin: Institut Kirche und Judentum, 1993.

Bahur, Eliyahu. *Sefer ha-Bahur*. Rome, 1519.

———. *Sefer ha-Tishbi*. Isny, 1541.

Baron, Salo. *History and Jewish Historians*. Philadelphia: Jewish Publication Society of America, 1964.

Baumgarten, Jean. *Introduction to Old Yiddish Literature*. New York: Oxford University Press, 2005.

Burnett, Stephen G. "Distorted Mirrors: Antonius Margaritha, Johann Buxtorf and Christian Ethnographies of the Jews." *Sixteenth Century Journal* 25, no. 2 (1994): 275–87.

———. *From Christian Hebraism to Jewish Studies: Johannes Buxtorf (1564–1629) and Hebrew Learning in the Seventeenth Century*. Leiden: Brill, 1996.

———. "Hebrew Censorship in Hanau: A Mirror of Jewish-Christian Coexistence in Seventeenth-Century Germany." In *The Expulsion of the Jews: 1492 and After*, ed. Raymond B. Waddington and Arthur H. Williamson, 199–222. New York: Garland, 1994.

Buxtorf, Johannes. *Judenschul*. Basel, 1603.

Carlebach, Elisheva. "Attributions of Secrecy and Perceptions of Jewry." *Jewish Social Studies* 2, no. 3 (1996): 115–36.

———. *Divided Souls: Converts from Judaism in Germany, 1500–1750.* New Haven, CT: Yale University Press, 2001.

———. "Jewish Responses to Christianity in Reformation Germany." In *Jews, Judaism and the Reformation in Sixteenth-Century Germany*, ed. Dean Phillip Bell and Stephen G. Burnett, 451–86. Leiden: Brill, 2006.

———. *Palaces of Time: Jewish Calendar and Culture in Early Modern Europe.* Cambridge, MA: Belknap Press of Harvard University Press, 2011.

Cohen, Mark R. "Leone da Modena's *Riti*: A Seventeenth-Century Plea for Social Toleration of Jews." *Jewish Social Studies* 34 (1972): 287–321.

———., ed. and trans. *The Autobiography of a Seventeenth-Century Venetian Rabbi.* Princeton, NJ: Princeton University Press, 1988.

de le Roi, J. F. A. *Die evangelische Christenheit und die Juden.* 3 vols. Karlsruhe und Leipzig: Reuther, 1884.

de'Rossi, Azariah. *The Light of the Eyes.* Ed. and trans. Joanna Weinberg. New Haven, CT: Yale University Press, 2001.

Deutsch, Yaacov. *Judaism in Christian Eyes: Ethnographic Descriptions of Jews and Judaism in Early Modern Europe.* New York: Oxford University Press, 2012.

———. "A View of the Jewish Religion: Conceptions of Jewish Practice and Ritual in Early Modern Europe." *Archiv für Religionswissenschaft* 3 (2001): 273–95.

Deutsch, Yaacov, Michael Meerson, and Peter Schäfer, eds. *Toledot Yeshu (The Life Story of Jesus) Revisited: A Princeton Conference.* Tübingen: Mohr Siebeck, 2011.

Diemling, Maria. "Anthonius Margaritha on the 'Whole Jewish Faith': A Sixteenth-Century Convert from Judaism and His Depiction of the Jewish Religion." In *Jews, Judaism and the Reformation in Sixteenth-Century Germany*, ed. Dean Phillip Bell and Stephen G. Burnett, 303–33. Leiden: Brill, 2006.

———. "'As the Jews Like to Eat Garlick': Garlic in Jewish-Christian Polemical Discourse in Early Modern Germany." In *Food and Judaism: Studies in Jewish Civilization*, vol. 15, ed. Leonard Greenspoon, Ronald Simkins, Gerald Shapiro, 215–34. Omaha, NE: Creighton University Press, 2005.

———. "Christliche Ethnographien über Juden und Judentum in der Frühen Neuzeit: Die Konvertiten Victor von Carben und Anthonius Margaritha und ihre Darstellung jüdischen Lebens und jüdischer Religion." PhD diss., University of Vienna, 1999.

Efron, John M. "Interminably Maligned: The Conventional Lies about Jewish Doctors." In *Jewish History and Jewish Memory: Essays in Memory of Yosef Hayim Yerushalmi*, ed. Elisheva Carlebach, John M. Efron, and David N. Myers, 296–310. Hanover, NH: Brandeis University Press, 1998.

Eisenmenger, Johann. *Entdecktes Judenthum*. 2 vols. Konigsberg, 1711.

Eisenstein, Judah David. *Ozar Vikukhim*. New York: J. D. Eisenstein, 1928.

Elyada, Aya. "'Eigentlich Teutsch?' Depictions of Yiddish and Its Relations to German in Early Modern Christian Writings." *European Journal of Jewish Studies* 4, no. 1 (2010): 23–43.

———. *A Goy Who Speaks Yiddish: Christians and the Jewish Language in Early Modern Germany*. Stanford, CA: Stanford University Press, 2012.

Faierstein, Morris. "Paulus Aemilius, Convert to Catholicism and Printer of Yiddish Books in Sixteenth-Century Augsburg." *Judaica: Beiträge zum Verstehen des Judentums* 71, no. 4 (2015): 349–65.

———. "The Yiddish *Humash* in the Sixteenth Century." Forthcoming in Ze'ev Gries festschrift. Carmel: Jerusalem, 2016.

Flusser, David. *Sefer Yosippon*. 2 vols. Jerusalem: Bialik Institute, 1978–80.

Fraenkel-Goldschmidt, Chava. *The Historical Writings of Joseph of Rosheim: Leader of Jewry in Early Modern Germany*. Leiden: Brill, 2006.

Grünbaum, Max. *Jüdischdeutsche Chrestomathie*. Leipzig: Brockhaus, 1882.

Haberman, Jacob H. "Moses Frankfurter." *Encyclopedia Judaica*, vol. 7, 98. Jerusalem: Keter, 1971.

Herford, R. Travers. *Christianity in Talmud and Midrash*. Hoboken, NJ: Ktav Publishing House, 1975.

Hominer, Hayyim. *Sefer Yosippon*. 4th ed. Jerusalem: Hominer, 1978.

Judah the Pious. *Sefer Hasidism*. Ed. R. Margulies. Jerusalem: Mosad Harav Kook, 1973.

Kaplan, Debra. *Beyond Expulsion: Jews, Christians, and Reformation Strasbourg*. Stanford, CA: Stanford University Press, 2011.

Karo, Joseph. *Shulchan Aruch*. Venice, 1565.

Katz, David S. "Shylock's Gender: Jewish Male Menstruation in Early Modern England." *Review of English Studies* 50, no. 200 (November 1999): 440–62.

Katz, Jacob. *From Prejudice to Destruction: Anti-Semitism, 1700–1933*. Cambridge, MA: Harvard University Press, 1980.

Kirn, Hans-Martin. *Das Bild vom Juden im Deutschland des frühen 16. Jahrhunderts: Dargestellt an den Schriften Johannes Pfefferkorns*. Tübingen: Mohr Siebeck, 1989.

Levitats, Isaac. "Oath More Judaico or Jurametum Judaeorum." *Encyclopedia Judaica*, 1302–3. Jerusalem: Keter, 1971.

Maher, Dr. Samuel. "Korrespondenz: Salomon Zebi, der Theriakolog." *Allgemeine Zeitung des Judentums* 23 (1846): 340–42.

Malkiel, David. "The Jewish-Christian Debate on the Eve of Modernity: Joshua Segre of Scandiano and His *Asham Talui*." *Revue des Etudes juives* 164, nos. 1–2 (2005): 157–86.

Mannheimer, S. "Samuel Friedrich Brenz." *Jewish Encyclopedia*, vol. 3, 370. New York: Funk and Wagnalls, 1901–6.

Martin, Ellen. *Die deutsche Schriften des Johannes Pfefferkorn: Zum Problem des Judenhasses und der Intoleranz in der Zeit der Vorreformation*. Göppingen: Kümmerle, 1994.

Matut, Diana. *Dichtung und Musik im frühneuzeitlichen Aschkenas*. 2 vols. Leiden: Brill, 2011.

McClintock, John, and James Strong. *Cyclopedia of Biblical, Theological and Ecclesiastical Literature*. Harper & Brothers: New York, 1870.

Meerson, Michael, and Peter Schäfer, eds. and trans. *Toledot Yeshu: The Life Story of Jesus*. Tübingen: Mohr Siebeck, 2014.

Menahem ben Zerach. *Zedah la-Derekh*. Ferrara, 1554.

Mieses, Josef. *Die älteste gedruckte deutsche Uebersetzung des jüdischen Gebetbuches a. d. Jahre 1530 und ihr Autor Anthonius Margaritha: Eine literarhistorische Untersuchung*. Vienna: R. Löwit, 1916.

Perles, Joseph. "Bibliographische Mittheilungen aus München." *Monatsschrift für Geschichte und Wissenschaft des Judentums* 25 (1876): 350–75.

Pettegree, Andrew. *The Book in the Renaissance*. New Haven, CT: Yale University Press, 2010.

Rosenthal, Judah. "Anti-Christian Polemical Literature" [Hebrew]. *Areshet* 2 (1960): 130–79; 3 (1961): 433–39.

Scharbach, Rebecca. "The Ghost in the Privy: On the Origins of Nittel Nacht and Modes of Cultural Exchange." *Jewish Studies Quarterly* 20 (2013): 340–73.

Schaudig, Wilhelm. *Geschichte der Stadt und des ehmaligen Stiftes Feuchtwangen*. Feuchtwangen: Sommer & Schorr, 1927.

Scholem, Gershom. "The Idea of the Golem." In *On the Kabbalah and Its Symbolism*, 158–204. New York: Schocken, 1965.

Schreckenberg, Heinz. *Bibliographie zu Flavius Josephus*. Leiden: Brill, 1968.

———. *Die christliche Adversus-Judaeos-Texte und ihr literarisches und historisches Umfeld (1–20 Jh.)*. 3 vols. Frankfurt am Main: Peter Lang, 1982–94.

Shamash, Juspa. *Ma'aseh Nissim*. Amsterdam, 1696.

Shapiro, Marc. "Torah Study on Christmas Eve." *Journal of Jewish Thought and Philosophy* 8 (1999): 319–53.

Shmeruk, Chone. "Yiddish Literature Beyond the German-Speaking Area." In *Yiddish in Italia: Manuscripts and Printed Books*, ed. Chava

Turniansky and Erika Timm, 205–8. Milan: Associazione Italiana Amici dell'Universita di Gerusalemme, 2003.

Shtif, Nochem. "Michael Adam's Three Yiddish Books" [Yiddish]. *Filologishe Shriftn* 2 (1928): 135–68.

Shulvass, Moses. "Ashkenazim in Italy." In *Between the Rhine and the Bosporus: Studies and Essays in European Jewish History*, 158–83. Chicago: College of Jewish Studies Press, 1964.

———. *The Jews in the World of the Renaissance*. Leiden: Brill, 1973.

Steinschneider, Moritz. *Catalogus codicum hebraeorum bibliothecae academiae Lugduno-Batavae*. Leiden: Brill, 1858.

———. *Catalogus Librorum Hebraeorum in Bibliotheca Bodleiana*. Berlin: Friedlander, 1852–60.

Stern, Selma. *Josel of Rosheim: Commander of Jewry in the Holy Roman Empire of the German Nation.* Philadelphia: Jewish Publication Society, 1965.

Stow, Kenneth. "The Church and the Jews: From St. Paul to Paul IV." In *Bibliographical Essays in Medieval Jewish Studies: The Study of Judaism Volume II*, 109–65. New York: Ktav, 1976.

Urbach, E. E. ed. *Arugat ha-Bosem*. 4 vols. Jerusalem: Mekizei Nirdamim, 1938–63.

Walton, Michael T. *Anthonius Margaritha and the Jewish Faith: Jewish Life and Conversion in Sixteenth-Century Germany*. Detroit, MI: Wayne State University Press, 2012.

Weil, G. E. *Elie Levita: Humaniste et massorete (1469–1549).* Leiden: Brill, 1963.

Weinreich, Max. *History of the Yiddish Language*. 2 vols. New Haven, CT: Yale University Press, 2008.

Yudlov, Isaac. *Ginzei Yisrael*. Jerusalem: Jewish National and University Library, 1985.

Zacuto, Abraham. *Sefer Yuhasin ha-Shalem.* Ed. Herschell Filipowski. London, 1857.

Zinberg, Israel. *History of Jewish Literature: Old Yiddish Literature from Its Origins to the Haskalah Period*, vol. 7. Cincinnati: Hebrew Union College Press, 1975.

Index of Citations

Text citations of chapter and verse appear in boldface, followed by its chapter and paragraph location in the *Theriak*.

I. Hebrew Bible

II. Intertestamental Works

III. New Testament

Rabbinic Citations
(Texts are cited in alphabetical order)

IV. Targum

V. Mishnah

VI. Babylonian Talmud

VII. Jerusalem Talmud

VIII. Midrash

IX. Medieval And Early Modern Works (Jewish and Christian)

General Index

CPSIA information can be obtained
at www.ICGtesting.com
Printed in the USA
LVOW03*1218121016
508384LV00003B/4/P

9 780814 342480